Princeton Review.com

WORD SMART JUNIOR

Build A Straight-A Vocabulary

by Hayley Heaton
and the Staff of The Princeton Review

3rd Edition

Random House, Inc.,
New York

The Princeton Review, Inc.
2315 Broadway
New York, NY 10024
Email: bookeditor@review.com

ISBN 978-0-375-42871-5

VP Test Prep Books; Publisher: Robert Franek
Editor: Adam O. Davis
Executive Director of Print Production: Scott Harris
Senior Production Editor: M. Tighe Wall
Illustrations: Jeff Moores

Printed in the United States of America.

9 8 7 6 5 4 3

ACKNOWLEDGMENTS

I would like to thank my editor, Adam Davis, and The Princeton Review for the opportunity to write such a fantastical and educational story. Also, I'd like to acknowledge Berle, Russ, Pattie, and Amber Heaton, Christie Haynes, Jeff, Tisha, Aidan and Ian Eggleston, Cate Peebles, Siobhan Cimenera, and Mark Hamilton for their fervent support and inextinguishable kindness.

CONTENTS

INTRODUCTION

INTRODUCTION

If you're like most students, you've probably been learning new vocabulary words in school for years. Each week your teachers assign a new list of words and then you have to look them up in the dictionary and write down their definitions. You might even have to use the words in a sample sentence. You might like doing this or you may hate it, but do you ever consider why you're doing it?

Well, simply put, having an expansive vocabulary will help you succeed in high school, college, and far beyond, and the best way to gain such a substantial arsenal is to learn new words in their proper context.

HOW THE BOOK WORKS

Word Smart Junior was written to help you learn vocabulary words as agreeably as possible by reading them in an entertaining and educational context. The book follows the story of The Cat, a spy on the trail of Asha Bloom, Little Lola, and Dr. Science, a group of infamous villains in pursuit of The Green Dragon.

There are around 700 different vocabulary words included in this book. When one of them appears for the first time it will be in bold face (**just like this**). If you read a word you're not sure of, try to figure out its meaning within the context of the sentence. A good wordsmith is a good sleuth—someone who can use clues from within a sentence to figure out what a particular word means. That said, if all else fails, there's a glossary in the back of the book that will give you a definition of each word, along with including it in a sample sentence. Try not to look up a word unless you absolutely have to, just enjoy each chapter and then go back and look up the words you didn't know.

DOING THE QUIZZES

There are quizzes at the end of each chapter to further help understand the words you've read. There are also answer keys to each quiz in the back of the book. (Don't peek!) If you miss something on the quiz look up the word in the glossary, and try using it in a sentence of your own. You should also go over the pronunciation guide at the beginning of each entry in the glossary since you'll definitely want to know how to pronounce each word properly before you use them.

That's about all you need to know. Now you can start reading, learning, and impressing everyone you know with your fabulous new vocabulary. Get going, Smarty Pants!

CHAPTER 1
A View to a cat

Hello there. I know that the **representation** to the left makes me appear as if I'm a loveable housecat who enjoys a good read, but the truth is to the **contrary**, my friends. I am a top-notch **practitioner** of **espionage**. In other words, I'm a spy.

I've been a spy for as long as I can remember. One **frigid** morning as I was taking in a bit of fresh air at my favorite park a woman approached me. She was wearing the most **ornate** dress I'd ever seen. It was made of gold silk and sewn with violet thread. The collar and sleeve cuffs were made of a very convincing **faux** fur and there were hundreds of small, green buttons forming a **parallel** line down her back. Her hat and handbag were both made of used, blue furniture **upholstery.** I later discovered her strange mode of dress was all part of a grand plot to overthrow a rather greedy **bureaucracy**.

The woman approached me and mysteriously asked me to take her handbag. I was clearly left **aghast** by her request. I'm not at all used to holding ladies' **accessories** and, to be quite honest, I wasn't sure that it would go well with my shoes. She then begged me, saying "I'm in a great deal of **jeopardy**. You've simply got to help me." Then adding, "The fate of the world depends upon it."

What else could I possibly do but follow her instructions? She told me to take her handbag and wait for her behind the fourth tree to the left of the park entrance. I waited for ages until finally she returned. She took back her handbag and quietly said, "Take this package."

Most spies will tell you that they didn't choose the life of being a spy, but rather that the life chose them. And that is exactly what happened to me. When I opened the package I found a tuxedo and a flight **itinerary** with a note inviting me to a party in Switzerland. I never saw the strangely-dressed woman again.

OOOOOOOOOOOO

I know you're wondering how I went from being an ordinary **civilian** to being a spy just like that. Obviously, it didn't happen that quickly. When I arrived in Switzerland I found myself at spy school where I learned every trick of the trade. When I started my studies I was completely awkward. I couldn't for the life of me figure out how to unfold, read, and then re-fold a map. I always put my see-in-the-dark night goggles on upside-down. I was completely terrible at rock climbing. And I couldn't prepare a **soufflé** to save anyone's life, let alone my own.

Despite making **blunder** after blunder the important thing was that I kept trying. After a few months of **intensive** study I started to succeed. Not only could I rock climb, but I no longer needed a harness. Eventually, I didn't need goggles to see in the dark or silly, little maps. And my **culinary** skills were far superior to those of anyone else in the school. I'd learned and practiced all the spy **etiquette** I was presented with, but I still hadn't yet learned my most important lesson. I hadn't yet learned to **adapt**.

Soon enough though, I had graduated. In a mere few months I'd gone from awkwardly hiding behind a tree and holding a purse to being able to blend in with any crowd. **Despite** my confidence, however, I knew that I'd be **obliged** to learn many more rules and lessons in the field. And, boy, did I learn them.

ooooooooooooo

The first and **foremost** rule of being a good spy is having a fantastic disguise. As you can see, I'm disguised as a cat. I've found this to be my most successful disguise to date, because no one ever suspects a cat of spying. I once made the mistake of dressing up like a cow. My **bovine** appearance made everything incredibly awkward. I couldn't see, I couldn't hear, and I couldn't crawl through any small spaces. And the tail kept getting stuck in elevator doors, so I always had to take the stairs. I'm sure you understand how having to walk up endless flights of stairs dressed as a cow could present a problem. I didn't know how to control those bulky **limbs**.

Before I perfected my **feline** disguise I tried various other means of **camouflaging** my appearance. The time I tried just a simple **goatee** and feather boa I was **denounced** in front of a stadium full of soccer fans. A riot broke out and I barely made it out of Brazil alive. And when I tried a **canine** costume my ankles started to **chafe** just before I was taken **captive** by a group of **renegade** librarians. Librarians may appear as if they're cool, calm, quiet, and collected all of the time, but let me **assure** you, they can get rowdy and surprisingly violent if they think you're threatening to break into their library's rare books room. It wasn't until I settled on the **chic** disguise of a cat that I really started **flourish** as a spy. Not only does the disguise offer an **insurmountable** amount of agility, but I also find that it keeps me nice and cozy in cold weather, so much more so than regular spy clothing. Try staying warm in a pinstripe suit in Antarctica—it just doesn't work.

Another very important **component** of being a spy is having an **alias**. I have several: Kitty Kitty Bang Bang, Cat Man Do, Chuck, the list goes on…but my all-time favorite is, The Cat. Why is it my favorite? Because everyone knows that cats have nine lives. The most **essential** part of acquiring a name like The Cat is keeping it simple. You don't want something like Big Bertha or Scissor Legs; those are too specific. No, you want something **austere**, but not **banal**. It has to promote both a sense of **aversion** and **esteem**.

How did I get my alias? It's a rather funny **anecdote** involving a bag of kitty litter and a car full of clowns. You see, I was setting up a net in an abandoned pet store called The Scratching Post. It was, at the time, the known headquarters for a group of murderous clowns, and I wanted to catch them. As I didn't want to get caught while setting up the net, I spread a layer of kitty litter on the floor that would alert me with a scratching sound if anyone stepped on it. I was hoping to get in and out without an incident, but the clowns arrived and the second one of their big shoes hit the ground

I was warned. Of course, they were curious about the sound underneath their feet. "What's that noise?" the clown with the polka-dot necktie yelled.

"I don't know, turn on the lights," the clown with the ridiculously large trousers shouted in reply.

Then, the third, slightly smarter clown with an IQ of nearly 100 bent down and said, "I think it's kitty litter. There's kitty litter all over the floor."

"But why?" asked the clown with the polka-dot necktie.

"Yeah, how come there's kitty litter all over the floor?" chimed in the clown with ridiculously large trousers.

"I don't know," answered the smarter clown with the IQ of nearly 100. "We haven't even got a cat."

"Oh, yes you do," I yelled triumphantly as I jumped from my hiding place, "and you're all under arrest." With one tug of my hand I pulled the net around the three clowns. The clown with the polka-dot necktie and the clown with the ridiculously large trousers surrendered in mere seconds, but the smarter clown with the IQ of nearly 100 wasn't willing to go without a fight. Despite being trapped in a net, he thought that he could get away with being **gruff**.

"You won't get away with this, Cat," he screamed as he tried to wiggle free from the net. "You'll be sorry you ever dared to capture me! When I escape from this net I am going to skin you alive!"

"But you can't skin The Cat," said the clown with ridiculously large trousers.

"Yeah," agreed the clown with the polka-dot necktie, "he's The Cat!"

"Well, The Cat is going to be sorry one day," threatened the smartest clown of the three. "Maybe not today, but someday."

Of course, I wasn't sorry. I was happy. Not only had I captured a group of ruthless villains, but I'd also received a wonderful new alias.

OOOOOOOOOOOO

A lot of spies talk to each other in what seems like an absolutely nonsensical language, but it's actually a clever spy **jargon** used so that others can't understand what we're talking about. Of course, you can understand why that's important. I shouldn't do this, but I'm going to share with you how the code works. It's all based on a system of **synonyms** and **antonyms**. For example, let's say that I want to tell another spy that I'm hungry and want to eat some fruit. I'd say, "The fruit in the fruit bowl is lovely this time of year." If the spy agreed with me they'd respond, "Yes, apples are in season." The words, "fruit" and "apples" are similar. In other words, they are synonyms. If the spy didn't agree with me, they'd say, "I prefer asparagus." As you know, asparagus is not a fruit, it's a vegetable and fruits and vegetables aren't the same, so that makes them antonyms rather than synonyms. It's tricky, I know.

The first time I tried talking in spy code was an absolute mess, and the whole mission turned out to be a giant **kerfuffle**. I was sitting at a café in Alaska waiting for a piece of halibut and reading a local newspaper when a man with a bushy mustache came near me and whispered, "The salmon is undercooked and spawning early this year."

As I was trying to be polite I responded, "Thank you for that information, sir. I appreciate it. You'll be happy to know I ordered the halibut."

The man looked at me strangely and tugged at his mustache a few times before saying, "Rainbow trout do not swim in these waters."

"But, sir, I ordered the halibut," I insisted.

My response only seemed to upset him and in a slightly angry tone he said, "You cannot swallow a gold-fish."

"I will not be swallowing any goldfish, you idiot, I ordered the halibut," I whispered in an irritated voice. By this time all I wanted was a plate with a piece of halibut, some steamed vegetables, and maybe a lemon wedge. I didn't care about salmon, rainbow trout, or goldfish. I was annoyed by this crazy man with the mustache who was overly obsessed with different kinds of fish. It didn't dawn on me that he was trying to give me a message which is most likely why I said, "Sir, this is a café not the aquarium. Are you lost? Perhaps the kind waitress can assist you with directions. Now would you excuse me please, I'm waiting for some halibut and a big boat."

"You imbecile," he finally blurted out, "the boat you were expecting left 20 minutes ago while you were waiting for your halibut and now we'll never find that shipment of stolen caviar!"

I jumped up to look out the nearest window. Wouldn't you know it, the boat I was waiting for had sailed out of the harbor with the stolen shipment of caviar and the suspects, but just then my halibut arrived with a lemon wedge.

OOOOOOOOOOOO

Like all good spies, I have had a **nemesis** or two over the years. However, most of my sworn enemies had been captured, all but three anyway.

I find that I have a great deal of **suspicion** when it comes to people wearing sunglasses, which is all due to one person in **particular**. Her name is Asha Bloom. It is said that Asha's **ancestors** are part of the Peloponnesian **monarchy**, but her royal blood doesn't stop her from being an **infamous** crook. Ms. Bloom has very expensive tastes, and when she wants something she doesn't save up her allowance like you and I. Instead, she plots and schemes to steal things. She's normally fond of jewelry and often has her sunglasses **encrusted** with stolen jewels, but that's not all she likes. Asha is also known for other forms of **debauchery**. I once heard that Asha was so **enamored** with the pet leopard of a French Canadian **dignitary** that she used a special **concoction** made with three crushed rubies to **intoxicate** the poor creature. Naturally, the leopard began to **hallucinate** and was **duped** into running away with Ms. Bloom.

The second **culprit** goes by the name of Little Lola and frequently **dons** a baseball cap. She may appear to be a **timid** thing, but I assure you, she is not. I've heard her say that she wears the cap so that she doesn't look **conspicuous**, but she really wears it to hide large amounts of **loot**.

Little Lola **hails** from a rather **rustic** mountain town west of the Mississippi River and grew up the youngest member of 13 children. Faced with the **plight** of flipping burgers for a lifetime, Lola turned to a life of crime at an **impressionable** age.

And now, although I absolutely **loathe** having to do this, it is my duty to tell you about Dr. Science. Dr. Science started out as a member of a top secret **clergy** who were known for the **forgery** of historical documents and priceless works of art. There's no telling how many paintings and sculptures he's **duplicated** and replaced. His replica statue of *The Venus de Milo* caused an international scandal when it was found **in lieu** of the real one doing a headstand in the Louvre. I'm **dismayed** to say that making fakes isn't his only skill. In fact, there really is no telling what Dr. Science can or will do. He's been involved in plots to transplant all penguins from their natural habitats to inner city zoos. He laid plans to dig a sink hole underneath the Parliamentary building in Victoria, Canada. He always hogs the popcorn at the movies. He stole a lifetime supply of multivitamins from a retirement home in Cape Cod. He's been spotted among whales with a harpoon in his hand. He kidnapped a movie star and held her for ransom. He left a candy bar wrapper on top of the Empire State Building. He's mugged a golfer and a tennis player. He poured food dye in the canals of Venice. He filled the Paris Metro with bubbles. He covered Buckingham Palace in toilet paper. He never finishes his vegetables and gives chocolate to dogs. He's robbed at least seven banks in

Texas. He hates skateboards. His hair is always notably **unkempt**. And he's been in **cahoots** with Asha Bloom and Little Lola.

OOOOOOOOOOOO

Most recently, I've been on a case in Northern Ireland tracking a well-known **plagiarist** who would claim that he was **ad-libbing** when really he was copying the poems of William Shakespeare. Having just put him behind bars, I was feeling a slightly **peckish** and decided to stop for a cup of tea and some cakes. Cakes are one of my few weaknesses, especially when they come with a cup of tea. So, off I went to Aunty Claire's Tea Shoppe feeling quite satisfied and quite hungry. I asked Aunty Claire for a table near the window and she warned me against sitting there. "There's something very strange happening over there, but you know me, I like to keep my mind on my own affairs." I looked near the window and saw a man in a white lab coat with incredibly messy hair, a woman wearing expensive looking sunglasses, and a waitress in a baseball cap. "You'll have to excuse me," Aunty Claire said, "our new waitress likes to gab a little too much with the customers." With that she was stomping toward the table near the window and I had to seat myself.

As soon as I sat down and saw her face, I knew that the new waitress Aunty Claire was talking about was Little Lola, but I had no idea why such a criminal mastermind would **feign** being a waitress in a small tea shop. When I looked more closely at the customers and realized that they were none other than Asha Bloom and Dr. Science, I came to conclude that Aunty Claire was right; something strange was going on over there. I wasn't sure what it was, but I was determined to find out.

It was clear to me that I could not arouse any suspicion, so I ordered my cakes and tea from Aunty Claire and began to **eavesdrop** on what was going on at the table over by the window. It was almost impossible for me to hear what Asha, Little Lola, and Dr. Science were discussing, so I had to take slightly more drastic measure. Just then I remembered that I keep a wonderful, little device in my briefcase that looks like a crumb. If I could get that device closer to the table then I'd be able to hear what was going on. **Nonchalantly**, I started to rummage around until I found the device, and just as I was trying to figure out how to get the device over near Asha, Little Lola, and Dr. Science, I sneezed and the crumb flew out of my hand and right under their table. Success!

"Did you get my note?" Dr. Science asked Asha.

"Of course I got it, you dimwit. How else would I be meeting you here?"

"Why didn't I get a note," Little Lola chimed in. "All I got was a lousy phone call. You never write me notes."

"Pipe down, Lola, and pretend to do your job," demanded Dr. Science. "I need to talk to Asha about The Green Dragon." Little Lola disappeared into the kitchen.

"Alright, Dr. Science, where is it? Where is The Green Dragon," Asha asked greedily.

"I can't tell you just yet, Asha, but follow the instructions on this note and I will meet you soon," Dr. Science whispered as he handed Asha a note tied with a green satin ribbon. He then bit the head off a gingerbread man, smiled **menacingly**, and left Aunty Claire's Tea Shoppe in a rush. Asha **discreetly** untied the ribbon and began to read the note when she was rudely interrupted by Little Lola.

"What did he tell you? Did he have The Green Dragon with him?"

"No, you **ignoramus**. He knows where it is and we've got to join him to find it. Now go and get your things packed up so we can blow this joint. And don't forget your baseball cap—we're going to need it to hide The Green Dragon."

Little Lola left quickly and began gathering up her things while Asha took out her compact mirror and admired herself. It wasn't until after she had reapplied her lipstick that Asha realized the note and her cakes had been removed from the table by Aunty Claire. When Little Lola returned to the table Asha looked at her slightly panicked.

"I can't find the note Dr. Science gave me, Lola."

"What do you mean, Asha? He just gave it to you."

"I know, but it's gone now. I guess it's not that important, I remember what it said. Now get a move on, Lola, this place is starting to bore me."

The two of them got up and left. Luckily, the note was still in Aunty Claire's Tea Shoppe. All I had to do was find it. I glanced under the table near the window to see if I could spot the green satin ribbon with which the note was tied, but it wasn't in sight. It was then that I noticed Aunty Claire had a green ribbon tied around her finger.

As she approached my table all I could do was concentrate on the green ribbon, so it startled me when she asked me if I'd like another piece of cake. "Oh, no thank you, Aunty Claire," I said. Then, trying to change the subject, I asked, "Have you forgotten something recently?"

"I certainly hope not," she said. "Why do you ask?"

"I was just noticing that you had that lovely, green ribbon tied around your finger. Sometimes when people are trying to remember something they tie a string around their fingers."

"Oh, of course, silly me! I just tied this around my finger a few moments ago. It's such a pretty color that I'd wear it as a ring for the day. It was wrapped around some little note, but I just threw that in the trash," Aunty Claire replied.

"It is a very lovely color, Aunty Claire. It goes so well with your eyes."

"Oh, you old sweet talker, let me get you another piece of cake, or at least a cup of tea."

"That's really very kind of you, Aunty Claire, but I'm quite **satiated**. Let me help you clean up." I picked up my tea cup and brushed away the crumbs from the table top and followed Aunty Claire into her cozy tea shop kitchen. There it was, on top of the little trash basket, the note Dr. Science had written to Asha Bloom. I needed to create another distraction so that Aunty Claire wouldn't think it was odd that I was going through her trash. Suddenly, I dropped my tea cup and sent it crashing to the floor.

"My goodness, I can be so clumsy sometimes. I'm terribly sorry. If you show me your broom, I'll gladly clean up this mess."

"That isn't necessary. Tea cups break by the dozen around here," Aunty Claire said trying to put me at ease.

"Aunty Claire, I really must insist on cleaning up this mess. I'd feel absolutely terrible if I just left it here. Now, where do you keep your broom?" Aunty Claire smiled sweetly at me as she handed me her old broom and dust pan. Even though I absolutely hate sweeping I swept the mess, and as I dropped the broken little pieces of china in the trash can I stole the note without anyone noticing. Sometimes a spy has to do what a spy has to do.

Dear Ms. Bloom,

If you want to tame The Green Dragon you'll have to meet the elephant with a memory like an elephant. Take a train to the Jolly Old, you'll find him in the Menagerie.

Yours truly,
Dr. Science, M.D., Ph.D., Esquire

Clearly, what this spy now had to do was get out of Aunty Claire's Tea Shoppe and read the note Dr. Science had written Asha Bloom as quickly as possible. And that is just what I did. I put the note in my pocket, thanked Aunty Claire for the lovely cakes, and apologized once again for breaking her tea cup, and as soon as I left I hid behind a large tree and read the note. It said:

Obviously, my three foes were headed to a place where there'd be a lot of animals, but what was I to make of the phrase, "the Jolly Old?" I knew I'd heard it or seen it somewhere before, but I couldn't remember exactly where. I suddenly remembered and took out the necktie I keep in my briefcase. I read the label closely,

Smith & Sons, Making Jolly Old neckties since 1907, London, England. "That's it," I said to myself. "They're going to London to meet the notorious Elephant King, and I'd better get there before they do."

Relationships

Decide what type of relationship the words below have to each other. If the words have similar meanings, write "S" next to the pair of words. If they have different or opposite meanings, write "O" next to the words.

1. satiated :: hungry
2. duplicated :: resembling
3. encrusted :: covered
4. alias :: nickname
5. etiquette :: rudeness
6. ignoramus :: genius
7. discreet :: secret
8. enamored :: repulsed
9. concoction :: mixture
10. hail :: come from
11. timid :: bold
12. synonym :: opposite
13. antonym :: similar
14. feline :: cat like
15. chafe :: soothe

Relationships

Decide what type of relationship the words below have to each other. If the words have similar meanings, write "S" next to the pair of words. If they have different or opposite meanings, write "O" next to the words.

1. jargon :: gibberish
2. chic :: elegant
3. foremost :: least important
4. blunder :: mistake
5. faux :: real
6. itinerary :: schedule
7. obliged :: unaccountable
8. renegade :: follower
9. banal :: exciting
10. suspicion :: distrust
11. intoxicate :: confuse
12. rustic :: urban
13. dismay :: disappointment
14. nonchalant :: anxious
15. ornate :: showy

Fill in the Blank

Choose the word that best completes each of the following sentences.

1. Karen was very upset when she learned that the _____ had been torn on her favorite chair.

   a. page

   b. seam

   c. upholstery

   d. sheet

2. Josh felt that he could speak French very well after seven _____ years of study.

   a. awkward

   b. intensive

   c. frigid

   d. brave

3. Mark decided to grow a/an _____
    rather than keep his mustache.

    a. palm tree

    b. pony tail

    c. inch taller

    d. goatee

4. Walter found that discipline was a/an
    _____ part of being in the military.

    a. essential

    b. accidental

    c. upsetting

    d. incidental

5. If you're like most people in the morning your
    voice tends to be a little bit _____.

    a. caffeinated

    b. idiotic

    c. gruff

    d. silly

6. Gina was amazed when she heard the explosion across the street and the _____ it caused.

   a. peacefulness

   b. kerfuffle

   c. flood

   d. flat tire

7. England's _____ has been around for over one thousand years.

   a. fish and chips

   b. kingdom

   c. soccer league

   d. monarchy

8. Jennifer's _____ are descendants from a Roman general.

   a. ancestors

   b. trousers

   c. friends

   d. books

9. Alex put a glass against the door to _____ on his roommate's conversation.

   a. ignore

   b. record

   c. eavesdrop

   d. drop in

10. The sculpture of the Venus de Milo is a _____ of the goddess Venus.

    a. fake

    b. masterpiece

    c. departure

    d. representation

11. To bake a/an _____ you need a lot of eggs.

    a. omelet

    b. stew

    c. soufflé

    d. bagel

12. The duchess wore both a diamond necklace and bracelet as her _____.

   a. decoration

   b. accessories

   c. date

   d. ideas

13. If you want to be a chef, Paris, France is widely known as one of the best places to go to _____ school.

   a. French

   b. driving

   c. culinary

   d. night

14. It was chilly outside so Billy went back upstairs to _____ his jacket.

   a. see

   b. don

   c. join

   d. wash

15. It is not a good idea to go to a job interview with a/an _____ appearance.

a. unkempt

b. silly

c. impeccable

d. freaky

QUIZ #4

True or False

Decide whether the following statements are True or False about Chapter 1. If the statement is true, write a "T" next to it. If the statement is false, write an "F" next to it.

1. Dr. Science has committed an insurmountable amount of crimes.
2. Asha Bloom likes to hide her loot in a purse.
3. Little Lola is known for her forgery of famous works of art.
4. Asha Bloom was duped into joining forces with Dr. Science.
5. Dr. Science is an infamous crook.
6. Little Lola has an aversion to receiving notes rather than phone calls.
7. The Cat has a bovine appearance.

8. In order to be a good spy one must be able to adapt to any situation.
9. Asha Bloom, Little Lola, and Dr. Science are in cahoots with each other.
10. The Cat is very agile.
11. Little Lola never wears a baseball cap because she loves to be conspicuous.
12. Dr. Science began his criminal career in a clergy that duplicates fake artwork.
13. The Cat has many anecdotes about his start as a spy.
14. When The Cat feels peckish he enjoys tea and cakes.
15. Dr. Science is quite menacing.

Matching

Match each word on the left to a word with the similar meaning on the right.

1. contrary   a. shocked
2. practitioner   b. danger
3. frigid   c. opposite
4. parallel   d. prosper
5. espionage   e. professional
6. bureaucracy   f. even though
7. aghast   g. confirm
8. jeopardy   h. condemn
9. civilian   i. spying
10. despite   j. administration
11. camouflage   k. concealing
12. denounce   l. dog like
13. canine   m. aligned
14. assure   n. citizen
15. flourish   o. cold

Matching

Match each word on the left to a word with the similar meaning on the right.

1. component	a. wickedness
2. ad-lib	b. improvise
3. austere	c. hate
4. nemesis	d. easily influenced
5. particular	e. have visions
6. debauchery	f. instead
7. hallucinate	g. criminal
8. plight	h. enemy
9. dignitary	i. literary thief
10. impressionable	j. pretend
11. loathe	k. element
12. in lieu	l. dilemma
13. plagiarist	m. unfeeling
14. feign	n. specific
15. culprit	o. important person

CHAPTER 2
You Only Live Nine Times

There's nothing I hate more than waiting in line. It doesn't even matter where the line is—the grocery store, the video store, the bathroom, the spy cafeteria— I will certainly hate waiting in it. This is most likely why I was in such a bad mood in the **queue** at the taxi stand. I needed to get to London, and I needed to get there quickly in order to beat Ms. Asha Bloom and Little Lola to the Elephant King. As for Dr. Science, his whereabouts would have to be **ascertained** once I arrived at my destination.

As I finally made it to the front of the line at the taxi stand I heard a huge **clamor** and saw a hunk of metal speeding toward me at some unworldly **velocity**. I closed my eyes in fear and heard its breaks screech as it pulled up beside me. A voice yelled, "Where to, mate?" It was the voice of the driver.

"Are you responsible for this **monstrosity**?" I asked.

"Why, yes sir, I am. Now, are you comin' or stay-in'?" said the strange driver.

"I suppose I'm coming," I responded a little nervously.

"Hurry up then, mate. I haven't got all day."

I got into the clunker disguising itself as a taxi, put my seatbelt on and told the driver to take me to the nearest airport. Without a word the cab lurched forward and off we sped to Belfast.

"A lot of folks have been going to the Belfast airport," the driver said trying to make conversation.

"Is that so?" I asked.

"Yeah, I got this one fellow earlier wearing a ridiculous white coat and his hair looked like a rat's nest." When the driver mentioned the white lab coat and the messed up hair I knew he was talking about Dr. Science. Who else could it possibly be?

"Do you remember where he was going?"

"He talked on his cell phone most of the drive, but I do remember him mentioning something about hiding a green dinosaur where it'd be most obvious. I thought he was a complete nutter. I mean, who on earth thinks they can hide a green dinosaur? Everyone and their aunties would notice that!"

"The Green Dragon," I asked in a slightly **irked** tone.

"Yeah, that was it, The Green Dragon. But still, you can't hide a dragon, mate. It's impossible."

For the rest of the bumpy ride I **pondered** what Dr. Science may have meant by hiding The Green Dragon where it would be most obvious. Why didn't he give The Green Dragon to Asha Bloom in the tea shop? Why was he hiding it at all? And what on earth did the Elephant King have to do with any of this? Dr. Science was up to something, one of his old tricks again. Perhaps he was trying to **lure** Asha Bloom and Little Lola into **deliberately** stealing a phony while he ran off with the real Green Dragon.

There were so many theories swirling around in my head that it wasn't until we actually reached the airport that I remembered my upcoming **rendezvous** with Asha Bloom, Little Lola, and the unsuspecting Elephant King. I paid the driver and thanked him for the information he gave me. He looked at me like I'd said something unusual, but I had no time to explain, nor did I want to, so off I rushed into the Belfast airport with the taxi's rattling ringing in my ears.

○○○○○○○○○○○○

Ah, London! Home of fish n' chips wrapped in newspaper, fantastic rubber rain boots, and an Elephant King who will know where to find Dr. Science and The Green Dragon. The trouble with the Elephant King is that he's known for being **fickle**. One minute he's generously offering you a peanut and the next minute you're surrounded by his fierce gang of jackals who are well-trained in every martial art. I obviously had my work cut out for me, and after the **tedious** flight from Belfast I wasn't sure if I was up for it. I was feeling somewhat sleepy and all I really wanted to do was sit down at a pub and **binge** on a big plate of bangers and mash, but Asha Bloom and Little Lola were sure to be near and it was my job to catch them. This, of course, meant I had to find the Menagerie and beat them to the Elephant King.

Most big cities are broken up into neighborhoods and London is no exception. It has lots of little neighborhoods like Mayfair, Notting Hill, and Leicester Square, but unlike these neighborhoods, the Menagerie is not well known. In fact, it's practically invisible unless you know it exists. For centuries the Menagerie was ruled by a family of frogs. At first, they were very good rulers, but over time they became easy to take advantage of and it is because of their **lax** attitudes that the Elephant King was able **usurp** the throne.

The previous ruler, Frog King Taddeus III, was very fond of board games, especially chess. Some say that while the Frog King was in power he often challenged his subjects to defeat him at long games of chess, but none of them ever could. That is until one day an elephant took up the challenge. The elephant, however, told the Frog King he'd only play on one condition. "I will play a game of chess with you, Frog King, if you give up your kingdom to me when I win." The Frog King, being very good at chess and confident in his family's **longevity** on the throne, thought it would be an easy win, so he agreed. Unfortunately, it wasn't as easy as he originally thought. The game lasted for ten days with pawns moving from square to square and queens racing from side to side of the board. Eventually, the Frog King got angry and accused the elephant of trying to **sabotage** him. This upset the elephant and although he quit the game he swore to himself that one day he'd take over the Menagerie. For a time the Menagerie was peaceful. All the king's subjects went to and from their jobs. They had tea and cakes every afternoon at four o'clock. They enjoyed fish n' chips and watched plenty of soccer games. They did all this until one week in March when a gang of ruthless jackals started a crime spree. The Frog King didn't quite know how to handle the gang of jackals and appealed to everyone he knew. The jackals, however, were not at all **conciliatory**. They simply wouldn't give up their life of crime.

"I like stealing peoples' televisions," said the jackal who was best at kung-fu.

"Yeah, and I like taking old ladies' purses," said the jackal who could break cinder blocks with his forehead.

"Don't forget scaring little girls," added the jackal with a crooked snout.

"We love scaring little girls," the jackals all howled together.

The Frog King held meeting after meeting, conference after conference, but nothing was done. No one could think of a way to make the jackals **vacate** the Menagerie, no one except for the elephant.

While the Frog King Taddeus III was wasting his time trying to kick the jackals out of the Menagerie, the elephant was trying to negotiate with them. Eventually, the elephant and the gang of jackals reached an agreement. They would go to the Frog King and demand that the elephant be **dubbed** ruler of the Menagerie, and in return the elephant would give the jackals a health and fitness center complete with a hot tub and doggie run as well as making them all members of a police squad. It was **mutiny** and although the Frog King **resented** it, he had to step down and make the elephant king of the Menagerie.

There were a lot of welcome changes in the Menagerie once the elephant became the Elephant King. He gave the jackals their health spa and opened a public swimming pool. He also donated a lot of money to the arts and started a campaign to keep the neighborhood cleaner by installing a number of rainbow-colored trash cans on each corner. In return, everyone who lived in the Menagerie gave the Elephant King whatever he wanted. Eventually, this caused a problem since power can make some moody. This was exactly the case with the Elephant King: He had way too much power and all that power made him very moody.

⚫⚫⚫⚫⚫⚫⚫⚫⚫⚫⚫⚫

I'd like to offer you some advice: If you know that you're going to be traveling through London on foot to **foil** a plot, make sure you bring an umbrella. London weather isn't known to be dry which is why I wasn't surprised when I felt the first raindrop hit my head. Luckily, I found an old rolled-up newspaper and held it over my head like they do in the movies. It worked decidedly well for a time, but while an umbrella can be held up to help you see where you're going, a rolled-up newspaper cannot. It just gets soggier and soggier.

I made my way toward the Menagerie as best I could in the **foul** weather, but with my limited vision it was a bit difficult. It wasn't until I ran into one of the rainbow-colored trash cans that I knew I was close. I took the newspaper away from my head and looked around. The Menagerie wasn't at all what I expected. It was very quiet, not the **pandemonium** you'd expect to find entering a busy neighborhood. All the shops were closed. No one was walking around on the streets. Not a soul was swinging on the playground or eating grapes on any of the park benches. I decided it was proba-bly because of the weather, but **instinctually** felt that something was wrong. And boy was I right. Just as I'd thrown the newspaper into one of the bright trash cans I heard a rather **macho** voice say, "Just what do you think you're doing?"

"I was just throwing away this soggy newspaper," I replied looking to see where the voice was coming from.

"You can't throw away a newspaper. You have to recycle newspaper," the voice said.

"Oh, I'm terribly sorry. Could you point me in the direction of a recycling bin," I asked politely.

"It's too late for that, cat. You're under arrest. Bruno, take him and put him with the others." Suddenly, I saw a rather large jackal come toward me, and in seconds flat he had me in a hold that made me wince with pain. "Listen here," I protested, "this isn't necessary. I said I would recycle the newspaper. There's no need to put me under arrest."

"Can it, bub," the jackal apparently named Bruno said. "Just do as you're told and you won't get hurt." I didn't want to **undermine** Bruno's authority for fear of him breaking me into pieces, so I went along with him. As he **briskly** escorted me toward a group of jackals I told myself not to panic. I'd been in worse situations than this before. Being held prisoner by a group of jackals was nothing compared to a group of renegade librarians. I don't know if you know this, but renegade librarians are completely vicious. I was certain that once I was taken to the Elephant King I could talk my way out of this **skirmish**. However, I wasn't taken to the Elephant King, I was placed in a circle with three other prisoners. I looked around and saw that we were being guarded by a group of ill-tempered jackals whose heads were **adorned** with helmets and whose hands were

equipped with knives. Then I noticed who the other prisoners actually were. Not only was I surrounded by a bunch of **uncouth** jackals, but I was also surrounded by Asha Bloom, Little Lola, and Dr. Science. No matter how one looked at it, the situation did not **bode** well for any of us.

Although my fantastic cat disguise allowed me to remain **incognito**, I **hesitated** to introduce myself to my fellow captors. I knew who they were but they didn't have any idea who I was, and I wanted to keep it that way.

"What's with the cat?" Asha asked the jackal with the sharpest knife.

"None of your business, lady," replied the jackal.

"Who are you?" Asha asked me.

To keep my identity hidden from her I responded with a quiet "meow," as if I were some sort of **novice** who didn't know what he was doing. Due to Asha's **gullible** nature she believed me and my plan worked. She thought I was just a poor, little kitten who'd been abused by the terrible jackals. She had no idea that I was a secret agent out to thwart her efforts to steal The Green Dragon. Dr. Science, I'm afraid, didn't feel the same way.

"Asha, get away from that stupid cat. He's not our problem."

"But Dr. Science, he's so furry and cuddly. Can't we keep him?"

"Yeah, c'mon, Doc, look how sweet he is," added Little Lola.

"Such a sweet little kitten, let's get him a ball of string to play with, Lola," Asha said.

"What a great idea, Asha. Kittens love string. And hats, they love to wear hats. Let's get the furry little kitty a nice big bonnet."

"Yes, a nice big bonnet with ribbons and a wagon. We can pull him around in a wagon. Won't that be cute, Lola?"

"Totally cute. The cutest thing ever," Lola said coming closer and scratching behind my ears. "Dr. Science, where can we get a bonnet around here?"

"Have you two forgotten what we've come here for," Dr. Science whispered. "We're here to find the Elephant King so he can tell us where to find The Green Dragon. Now stop being so **trite**. We haven't got time for this. And by the way, that cat looks utterly **gross**. He's not cute at all."

Admittedly, I was a little offended by Dr. Science's opinion of my disguise, but at least he got me out of wearing a bonnet. And he was right, we all needed to find the Elephant King.

"We need to see the Elephant King," Dr. Science demanded.

"The Elephant King is on vacation," the jackal with the sharpest knife said.

"On vacation, that's a good one," said the jackal who was practicing his jump kicks while trying not to laugh too much.

"Yeah," said the jackal who liked ham sandwiches, "the Elephant King is **en route** to sunny Ibiza to catch some rays and go clubbing." The jackals all went wild with laughter.

"Who is in charge here?" an irritated Dr. Science asked.

"Who do you think? We are," said Bruno the jackal. "We're in charge and you're all going to rot in jail just like the Elephant King."

"Wait a minute," Asha finally said, "I thought you told us that he was on his way to the beach."

"Did I say the beach?" said the jackal who liked ham sandwiches. "I meant he's in prison. We've taken over the Menagerie and declared **martial law**."

The situation was quickly becoming **overwhelming**. There I was with fierce looking jackals on one side, masterminded criminals on the other, and about to be thrown into prison with the Elephant King. I needed to escape the jackals and rescue the Elephant King so that I could find out where The Green Dragon was located in order to keep it safe from Asha, Lola, and Dr. Science. I needed a miracle, but the best I could do was come up with a **spontaneous** plan. If I could sneak off without anyone noticing I could break into the prison and save the Elephant King. What I needed was another distraction. Unfortunately, I didn't have a teacup with me to break. I did, however, have my wits. I immediately crept up behind Asha Bloom and gave her a firm shove which knocked her into Little Lola. Lola assumed that it was Dr. Science who shoved her so she shoved him in return. Dr. Science **concluded** that Asha shoved him so he shoved her straight into the jackal who liked to watch baseball games, and in no time flat there was a full-out shoving, kicking, biting, and spitting battle with Asha kicking anyone she count and Dr. Science throwing the contents of his lab coat pockets everywhere. Thanks to this I was able to sneak away without being noticed.

●○○○○○○○○○○○

Prisons are typically very unpleasant places. I've never been to one I liked, and the Menagerie prison was no exception. I'd like to **omit** the details of what I saw and just tell you that I rescued the Elephant King without any problems, but that wasn't the case. It's just as hard to break into a prison as it is to break out of one.

The Menagerie prison sits on top of a large hill surrounded by a moat with ferocious crocodiles and piranhas. If you're able to make it past the treacherous swim and the long hike you've got to ambush the two guards who protect the front gate. I had no trouble with the guards—they were well past their **prime**. Once I was in the prison, however, things started to get a little complicated. None of the cell numbers in the prison were in **sequential** order. Cell number 1A was located on the seventh floor and cell number 3F was on the fifth floor. After running from floor to floor with jackals hot on my heels, I finally found a trap door that lead to a dungeon. It was dark and damp and smelled like rotten fish. I started to think that I'd never find the Elephant King. I was even worried that I wouldn't be able to escape and that I'd have to live the rest of my life running through hallways with jackals on my trail. I sat down on the cold stone floor and tried to collect myself and my thoughts. If I were a prison guard where would I put the Elephant King? I'd never find out if I gave up. I **resolved** to keep looking. It was too important not to. I stood up and hit my head on something hard. It must have made a loud sound because as I was rubbing it better I heard a voice. "Hello, is anyone there? Who are you? I say, is anyone there?"

"Maybe, who's asking?" I replied.

"This is the Elephant King. I demand that you let me out of this horrible cell. I am king of the Menagerie and holding me prisoner is illegal!"

I couldn't believe it. By some **quirk** of fate I'd found the Elephant King. "I'm here to help you your highness."

"If you help me escape, you will reap a very large reward."

"All I want, your highness, is some information," I said as I worked at picking the lock on the Elephant King's cell door.

"Information? What sort of information?"

"I need to know where The Green Dragon is located," I said as the door finally flew open. The Elephant King emerged looking less than kingly. His robes were dirty and his crown had been tarnished. "Are you all right," I asked.

"Yes, I'm quite fine. My **ego** is a little damaged, but I'm well enough. Thank you for helping me."

"You're welcome. Now what can you tell me about The Green Dragon?"

"I'm afraid I can't tell you much," the Elephant King replied. "The Green Dragon used to reside in my crown." He took off his crown and showed it to me. "As you can see, it is no longer there. I was tricked into selling it to a ridiculous looking hippie who told me that he would build a new yoga center in the Menagerie."

"Let me get this straight. You sold The Green Dragon to a hippie who promised you a yoga center?" I asked, more than a little shocked.

"Yes," the Elephant King said, "it's very important to be centered."

"Does anyone else know about this?"

"Just a man named Dr. Science who told me he could make a copy of The Green Dragon. You see, I was going to sell the fake to the hippie and keep the real one to myself, but I wasn't able to get the fake one in time. I was put in this prison before Dr. Science could get it to me."

"Who is this hippie? Where is he? You've got to tell me," I said trying to keep my voice from echoing.

"He calls himself Guru Doug and lives in Italy with his wife Linda."

"Where in Italy?"

"It's a strange little town north of Rome called Calcata," the Elephant King whispered.

"Does Dr. Science know about Guru Doug? Does he know he has The Green Dragon?"

"I'm afraid he might," the Elephant King said sadly. "I've lost The Green Dragon forever, haven't I?"

Just then we heard footsteps. The jackals were on to us. "Come on, your highness, we've got to get out of here." "There's a secret exit to the left."

"How do you know where the secret exit is?" I asked.

"I designed the prison," the Elephant King said. And with that we started running.

oooooooooooo

When the Elephant King and I finally made it to the secret passage, down the giant hill, and past the moat we saw a group hurrying toward us. There were four confused ostriches, a peace-loving panda bear, two hideous jackals, and three known criminals.

"Thank goodness you're free," the jackal with rotten teeth said.

"Thank goodness? Thank goodness indeed! It was your fault I've been rotting in that prison for the past three weeks. Take **heed**! All jackals are now known enemies to the citizens living in the Menagerie," the Elephant King announced. "And furthermore, anyone wearing a white lab coat or sunglasses will be brought in for questioning." The second they heard that, Asha Bloom, Dr. Science, Little Lola, and the jackals took to the hills. I was quite happy to be rid of the lot of them, but my satisfaction didn't last long since I knew well that'd I'd be seeing them again very soon.

Relationships

Decide what type of relationship the words below have to each other. If the words have similar meanings, write "S" next to the pair of words. If they have different or opposite meanings, write "O" next to the words.

1. queue :: line
2. usurp :: surrender
3. foil :: hinder
4. ponder :: wonder
5. instinctually :: intuitive
6. resent :: like
7. sequential :: out of order
8. equipped :: outfitted
9. ascertain :: reject
10. monstrosity :: mess
11. wince :: smile

Relationships

Decide what type of relationship the words below have to each other. If the words have similar meanings, write "S" next to the pair of words. If they have different or opposite meanings, write "O" next to the words.

1. velocity :: speed
2. undermine :: weaken
3. vacate :: fill
4. trite :: overused
5. spontaneous :: planned
6. skirmish :: fight
7. pandemonium :: peace
8. uncouth :: well-mannered
9. quirk :: oddity
10. rendezvous :: date
11. resolve :: determination

Fill in the Blank

Choose the word that best completes each of the following sentences.

1. A house with a nice view is said to be a _____ piece of real-estate.

   a. so-so

   b. lucky

   c. prime

   d. ugly

2. The number of birthday candles on Fred's cake seemed to _____ his party guests.

   a. cheer

   b. overwhelm

   c. sadden

   d. disgust

3. Jenny decided to _____ the story of how she crashed her bike into a tree because she was embarrassed.

   a. omit

   b. make up

   c. return

   d. confess

4. Even though Jim had taken piano lessons for a year he was still a _____.

   a. genius

   b. liar

   c. novice

   d. nice guy

5. The pirates on the boat were sick of their captain and decided to commit _____.

   a. treason

   b. mutiny

   c. fair play

   d. murder

6. Steven couldn't get a date because he was acting too _____.

    a. macho

    b. fast

    c. cold

    d. rigid

7. Kate tried to _____ people into liking her by buying them gifts.

    a. capture

    b. kick

    c. force

    d. lure

8. Kenneth's _____ was amazing considering he'd been sick so many times as a child.

    a. longevity

    b. addiction

    c. hearing

    d. temper

9. Sally's parents had a very _____ attitude towards discipline.

    a. shameful

    b. lax

    c. scientific

    d. warm

10. It _____ Mark to wait in line.

    a. troubles

    b. gladdens

    c. irks

    d. affects

11. Don't _____ to ask a question if you don't understand something.

    a. pretend

    b. forget

    c. remember

    d. hesitate

Matching

Match each word on the left to a word with the similar meaning on the right.

1. heed
2. gullible
3. gross
4. deliberate
5. fickle
6. en route
7. ego
8. dub
9. conciliatory
10. clamor

a. commotion
b. self-esteem
c. name
d. pay attention
e. temperamental
f. on the way
g. disgusting
h. easily tricked
i. on purpose
j. willing

Matching

Match each word on the left to a word with the similar meaning on the right.

1. sabotage   a. damage
2. tedious   b. end
3. reap   c. fast
4. adorn   d. collect
5. binge   e. boring
6. bode   f. eat
7. brisk   g. foretell
8. conclude   h. decorate

CHAPTER 3
For Feline Eyes Only

I once spent three months studying under a Guru whose entire **didactic** philosophy was based on not answering questions. He would beg a group of us to ask questions and when we asked them he would say, "That answer must come from within."

"From within what?" I'd ask him.

"Within every being there is an answer to every question," he'd reply leaving me utterly clueless. Despite his **eccentric** ways, I did enjoy his company quite a bit. He was a very good swimmer. Clearly, I doubted very much that I'd enjoy Guru Doug as much. After all, I was sure that he was a **fraud**.

Unfortunately, I arrived in Calcata at the very same time as that little gang of villains. In other words, when I finally found Guru Doug, I was met by Dr. Science, Asha Bloom, and Little Lola. We'd probably even taken the same flight, train, and bus. As unhappy as I was to be bunched together with the three of them, at least I knew I could keep my eyes and ears open for any strange behavior. They were just as surprised to see me there. In fact, when Asha saw me she said, "Look Lola, it's that pretty little kitty cat. It's followed us to Italy. Isn't that sweet?"

"Dr. Science, Dr. Science," Lola said jumping up and down. "The little kitty has come with us. Can we keep it now? Can we? It obviously likes us."

"What do I care about a **mangy** cat? I'm looking for a dragon—The Green Dragon. But we've got to find that dumb Guru first."

"Yeah, Lola, we have to find The Green Dragon, don't be so stupid," Asha said, trying to sound tough.

Lola apparently didn't care about looking stupid. She'd grown rather fond of me and bent down and whispered, "Don't worry, kitty, they'll get used to you and then you can join us on as many adventures as you like." I clearly couldn't respond to her. I couldn't tell her that I didn't want to join them on their criminal adventures or that what I really wanted to do was **eradicate** any chance they had at getting The Green Dragon.

I followed the three of them through a **labyrinth** of streets, shops, and hills until finally we reached the spot where Guru Doug was known to deliver his daily **bohemian** affirmations to whomever would listen. At first there were very few people gathered around, but as the sun got a little higher in the sky a crowd grew. All of them arrived with yoga mats and bottles of spring water and many of them were wearing necklaces made of green beads. Finally at **dusk**, a man arrived wearing a flowered bathrobe, a pair of pants that were far too short to reach his ankles, a pair of old sandals, a silly hat, and some wire-framed glasses.

"Greetings, my friends," the man who was obviously Guru Doug said as he held up his hands in a **cliché** gesture meaning peace. "Everyone please, leave your mats, it is time for our daily disco."

All of the people that had crowded around got up from their yoga mats and began to **gyrate** in the wackiest way I'd ever seen. First, one would invent some strange dance step and one by one they would **mimic** each other. One would claim she was a tree blowing in the wind, the next would say he was a fish swimming in a cool stream, and then another would claim he was a blade of grass being eaten by a sheep. As creative as their imaginations were, their movements were all very **redundant**. Their hips rotated in circles while they moved around Guru Doug and all the while he was shouting out, "Back and forth, to and fro, all day long we **ebb** and flow." Eventually, the crowd began to repeat what Guru Doug was saying and it was clear that they were under his control.

Once he had confirmed that this faction was under his spell Guru Doug took a pouch out of the left pocket of his hideous bathrobe. As he began to unpack what was in the pouch the crowd of people started **kowtowing** to him.

"Oh, Guru Doug," the woman with the pink yoga mat said, "if you let me see it I'll give you all my money."

"No, Guru Doug, let me see it first and I'll give you the watch I inherited from my French uncle," a man with **flimsy** cane called out as he tried to dance more carefully.

"I will give you a house," said a different man wearing a pair of tight leather pants.

"I will build you a castle," said a woman trying to balance on one leg.

Guru Doug held the pouch above his head and the crowd got so loud that you couldn't even understand what each of them was shouting out. It was as if they were in some kind of **cult** and Guru Doug was the leader. Suddenly, he put the pouch back in his pocket and everyone went silent **abruptly**. "You have all made very generous offers this evening," Guru Doug said loudly. "I shall accept each and every one of them in due time, but until then I must put The Green Dragon back where it belongs and we must continue our disco."

The crowd danced until they were completely **listless**. Many of them were so tired after their exertions that they spent the night right there on their yoga mats instead of in their beds. The scene totally **baffled** me. I took my leave and sat near what used to be a fountain to collect my thoughts. Obviously, Guru Doug had The Green Dragon, but why was he using it to trick people out of their belongings? Before I could ask myself anymore questions I noticed a woman approaching Dr. Science, Asha Bloom, and Little Lola. What with the commotion of Guru Doug's disco, I'd almost forgotten that they were there at all. I quickly got on my feet and hurried toward them so that I could hear what she was saying.

"Are you new in town?" the woman asked.

"Yes, yes, just tourists, you know," replied Dr. Science in a fake accent.

"Well then, let me welcome you. I'm Linda, Guru Doug's wife."

"Was he the guy in the funny robe?" Asha asked.

"Oh dear, I'm afraid that's my robe. He keeps it on to keep out the chill."

"But it's hot outside," Lola said to the woman.

Linda smiled at them and said, "I'm afraid you weren't meant to take that too literally. I was just joking with you. You see, Guru Doug has some strange practices that are sometimes hard to explain to visitors."

"Yes, we can see that," agreed Dr. Science in his fake accent. "I don't suppose you know where we could find a hotel."

"There's no need for a hotel here. All visitors stay with us. And it's your lucky night, because I've made some delicious vegetarian lasagna," Linda said.

As all of them wanted to get closer to Guru Doug they didn't argue with Linda about spending the night. After all, the closer they were to Guru Doug, the closer they were to The Green Dragon.

○○○○○○○○○○○○

I suppose that before I get any further along in my story I should tell you more about The Green Dragon and the many **myths** that surround it. Legend has it that in order to avoid becoming the victim of a ritual human sacrifice, a young, **vivacious** Incan girl fled her home in search of something to protect her. She wandered for days and days and finally, as she was suffering from **famine** and extreme **fatigue**, the young girl stopped to rest on a soft plot of ground. As she sat down she started to cry. "All is hopeless," she said to herself, "I will not find what I am looking for and I'm so tired." The cool, soft ground felt so comforting to the young girl that she laid down and curled up. Before she knew it she was dreaming. In her dream everything turned green. Her smile was green, her eyes had turned from brown to green, her dress was green, her feet were green, even her heart was green. When the young girl awoke she found that she felt totally refreshed and had absolutely no **anxiety**. She stretched and thought, "What an **extraordinary** dream! I feel so much better." As she got up from her soft sleeping spot on the ground and looked around she noticed that the rocky path she had used was now covered in a soft moss and it lead into a cave. The young girl decided to follow the path and made her way toward the stony entrance. Before too long the girl found herself **peering** into the mouth of the cave. As she looked in she saw something that was impossible for her to ignore, a brilliant green glow. What else could the young girl do? She simply had to find the source where the glow was coming from. Sadly, just as she stepped past the cave's **threshold**, the young girl fell **prey** to a bear and was never heard from again.

It was hundreds of years later when The Green Dragon was actually **excavated**, along with the girl's remains, by an archeologist by the name of Fredrick P. Honeycutt. When Honeycutt found the emerald in the cave it reminded him of a lizard so he named it The Green Dragon and took it on a tour around the world with other things he'd stolen from caves. The Green

Dragon was so beautiful that audiences began to make up stories about its powers. Some said that if you touch it with your left ring finger you'll be engaged within a month. Others said that if you throw it three times in the air and catch it three times in a row you're granted three wishes by an actual little dragon that is trapped inside it. But Honeycutt knew the truth: The Green Dragon's real power was its **allure**, and he used this to hypnotize people. He would get audiences to stare at The Green Dragon while speaking very softly to them until they were under his control. And then he would do silly things like manipulate audience members to act like monkeys.

Power can do strange things to people, much like it did to Honeycutt. The power he had with The Green Dragon made him unstoppable. If he had wanted to I'm sure he could have gotten people to commit all sorts of nasty crimes for him: **manslaughter**, theft, perhaps even **genocide**. There's not telling what could happen if The Green Dragon got into the wrong hands. Fortunately, for some time, The Green Dragon remained safe.

When Honeycutt died he wanted his daughter to **inherit** The Green Dragon so he left it to her as an **heirloom**. But he didn't leave it in the best condition; it was dull and grubby looking after years of overuse which is most likely why she sold it at an auction to a French woman named Sophie Marcel who liked to paint. Sophie used to leave it on her table and paint different objects on it like fresh fruit or her stuffed animals. Eventually, Sophie got tired of painting it and gave it to her niece who lived in England. Her niece was a **staunch** political activist who, in efforts to improve the living conditions of her neighborhood, donated it to the Frog King. However, instead of using The Green Dragon's powers to clean up The Menagerie, the Frog King had the emerald placed in his crown so that he could control the minds of his subjects and win more board games. When he took over the throne, the Elephant King also took over the responsibility of protecting The Green Dragon. And we all know what a poor job he did.

○○○○○○○○○○○○

Like I've said before, at times, it is very **convenient** to be disguised as a cat, for example, when following a gang of three criminals and a crazy hippie woman through the streets of Calcata, Italy. No one suspects you of following them and, in this case, they even welcomed me. Little did they know I was spying on them.

"We can't forget our little kitten friend," Lola said as they started to leave.

"Yes, yes, come along little kitty," Asha said patting her leg and signaling for me to follow them. So follow, I did. It was almost *too* easy.

When we arrived at Guru Doug and Linda's **abode** I could tell that Dr. Science, Asha, and Little Lola were all very **weary** from their travels. I, however, being blessed with the strength, agility, and **finesse** of a cat, was not the least bit tired. In fact, I remember feeling quite ready for whatever was to happen next, even if it happened to be a marathon. Of course, it wasn't a marathon—it was a dinner party.

Linda, Guru Doug's strange wife, led us from the front of the house and back into the kitchen. "This is where we all get together after the daily disco and make dinner," she started to explain.

"Wait, you all make dinner together? You don't just order take-out?" Asha Bloom asked in a **curt** and offensive way.

Not wanting to cause any trouble Dr. Science tried to smooth things over, "Asha isn't used to making her own dinner, I'm afraid. But we're all very interested in how things work around here. What can we help with? Perhaps Guru Doug could use a hand with the salad."

Asha Bloom and Little Lola were both horrified at the suggestion that they both help prepare dinner, but one look from Dr. Science helped **deter** any more complaints and they all got to work. Little Lola was put to work chopping carrots, Asha Bloom was in charge of boiling water for the pasta, and Dr. Science was sent to help a strangely dressed woman grate parmesan cheese. And I tried to pretend that I was a sweet and cuddly kitty so I could sneak around and spy on what was happening.

"You see," the strangely dressed woman started to say to Dr. Science, "you can't really have pasta without the cheese. That's why our job is the most important." Dr. Science just nodded politely and tried to think of a way to change the subject.

"Cheese, cheese, cheese, that's all you ever talk about, Diane," said a tall man with a small mustache.

"Why can't we talk about something interesting for a change?"

The tall man with the small mustache's remark was clearly meant to **reprimand** Diane, the strangely dressed woman, but she didn't pay him any mind.

"Cheese is very important. Without this cheese our pasta would be totally **bland**," Diana said.

"You can put other things on pasta besides cheese, you know," said the tall man with the small mustache as a **retort**.

I could have stayed closer to the cheese argument, but it was clear that I wasn't going to learn anything about the whereabouts of The Green Dragon if I did. Dr. Science and I had that in common, but unlike him, I wasn't stuck grating cheese—I could go look cute and cuddly somewhere else. And that's exactly what I did.

First, I went over toward where Asha was staring at a large pot, waiting for the water to boil. "Is there any way to speed this up," she asked a man wearing a green t-shirt.

"I'm afraid the only way to **expedite** boiling water is to not stare at it while it's heating up," he said.

"But that's the job they gave me," she replied.

"Perhaps you could **forgo** that for the time being and read me the recipe for spaghetti sauce from this cook book."

Asha thought that reading from a cook book was far more interesting that watching water get hot, so she agreed and began to read out loud, "You need tomatoes and garlic…"

The man wearing the green t-shirt started to **compile** the ingredients for the spaghetti sauce in a large pot as Asha read him more directions. It was clear that I wasn't going to get any information here either, so I decided to see what Little Lola was doing. Perhaps the three of them had decided to trade being criminals for being chefs.

As I approached Little Lola chopping carrots I noticed that both Guru Doug and Linda were no longer in the kitchen. In fact, I can't remember ever seeing Guru Doug in the kitchen at all. I realized then if I wanted to find The Green Dragon that I'd have to find Guru Doug first and this was the perfect time, as Dr. Science, Asha Bloom, and Little Lola were all stuck in the kitchen.

Sometimes when people are trying to be polite about someone else's house they'll say something like, "What a lovely, **modest** living room," or "My goodness, what a charming and **humble** little home you have." Guru Doug's house was neither modest nor humble. It was **vulgar**. As I sneaked through the rooms hoping to hear voices I noticed things like red velvet curtains with orange and yellow polka-dots, giant snow globes from places like Florida, piles and piles of gossip magazines, empty ice cream cartons, and a toilet made of solid gold. What kind of Guru needs a solid gold toilet? I'll tell you what kind, the kind that clearly **asserted** his **dogmatic** opinions in order to mislead people into giving him their money. What's worse is that he was using The Green Dragon to help him.

Just as I had reached a staircase made of seashells a voice rang out: "Linda, I am their **patriarch**, they'll do anything I say." The voice was Guru Doug's but I couldn't tell where it was coming from. I looked around and found that it was coming out of a vent made of little silver coins. Thankfully, I had **honed** my hiding skills in spy school, so it was easy for me to crouch down and listen without anyone noticing.

"But Doug, when we started this little commune you weren't supposed to be a father figure, you were supposed to be a **mentor** and now you're **dabbling** in strange hypnotizing exercises and **obscuring** the truth from these people—people who trust you. I just don't know who you are anymore." The voice was Linda's, and the two of them were having some sort of **quarrel**.

"I'm Guru Doug, that's who, and if you aren't **content** here you can leave."

"I don't want to leave. I want my husband back. Ever since you got that…that thing, you've been impossible to live with."

"Linda, I have no idea what you're talking about and why you have such **contempt** for something as precious as The Green Dragon."

"It's because it has turned you into a monster."

"The Green Dragon has done nothing of the sort. It's made me **omnipotent**."

"But you don't know everything, Doug. You don't even know how to make spaghetti."

"Can you in **earnest**, Linda, say that you hate the way we are living? Do you hate the curtains I picked out and that amazing gold toilet?

"It isn't the things I hate, it's how we got them. Your behavior has been absolutely **dubious** since you brought that Green Dragon into the house. It's the **bane** of my existence, and I can't **condone** what you're planning."

"Linda, I told you not to mention the plan when there are others in the house. You know it could ruin us if anyone heard what we've got cooking!"

"Maybe I should just go and tell them. I'll tell them all how you've committed **perjury** and that the promises you made them, the oaths you swore to them are never going to happen because you're giving The Green Dragon to Sidney Whitewall. You can't keep tricking these people into thinking that this emerald can solve all their problems."

"Are you trying to cause some kind of **exodus**, Linda? Do you want all those people in the kitchen to hear you and leave?"

"Yes, I'm sick of living a lie," Linda said and started to cry.

"Now there's **irony** for you. First you tell me you want to join a commune in Italy, then you tell me you want a gold toilet, then you tell me you like throwing dinner parties, and now you're telling me that's all a lie. I did this all for you, Linda. Now you can either sit there and **wallow** or you can join our guests and me for some spaghetti."

At this point, Guru Doug stormed out of a secret room that was well-hidden beneath the stairs and, to my surprise, ran straight into Dr. Science. I'd been so focused on listening to the conversation that I hadn't noticed him come into the room.

"Oh, excuse me," Dr. Science said, "I was just looking for your bathroom."

"It's down the hall and to the left," Guru Doug said politely, then left the room.

From the **pensive** look on Dr. Science's face I could tell that he'd overheard the whole conversation between Guru Doug and Linda which meant he knew all about Sidney Whitehall and The Green Dragon. As Dr. Science left to find the bathroom Linda came out of the secret room and took a deep breath in and then let it out slowly to calm herself. Then, she went into the kitchen to **presumably** check on the spaghetti and her guests.

After a very uncomfortable dinner of spaghetti and carrot salad, Linda, trying to be a good hostess, decided to offer Asha Bloom, Little Lola, and Dr. Science each a green beaded necklace. Little Lola readily accepted hers as she was rarely given presents. Asha took one but put it in her pocket instead of around her neck because it didn't match her outfit. Dr. Science tried to refuse the beads but ended up taking them in case they might be valuable. And I just tried to keep an eye on Guru Doug who was acting funny throughout the whole **ordeal**. I couldn't help but wonder what he was up to. Why did he need to give The Green Dragon to Sidney Whitehall and how was he going to get away with it? I'd find out soon enough.

○○○○○○○○○○○○

Shortly after midnight, after everyone had gone to sleep, I heard a door open and then close quietly. I then heard voices in the secret room where Guru Doug fought with his wife Linda earlier that evening, so I sneaked back to my original hiding spot near the vent to listen.

"Where's Mr. Whitehall? He was supposed to come himself," Guru Doug asked in a worried voice.

"Listen, pal, sometimes Mr. Whitehall gets busy and right now he's busy with his lady friend, so I came instead. Now hand it over," the other voice said in a threatening tone.

"Well, if he's not coming himself, what's the password? I'm not giving you The Green Dragon unless you know the password," Guru Doug demanded.

With an exasperated sigh the other voice whispered the password. Unfortunately, I was unable to hear what it was.

"All right, then, here it is, The Green Dragon. Can I assume that Mr. Whitehall will stop sending me those awful threats and agree that I no longer owe him any money?" asked Guru Doug.

"That's not my problem, pal, but as far as I'm concerned, you'll most likely never be hearing from us again, unless we decide to send you a postcard from Belize," the voice said with the same threatening **demeanor**.

So that's where The Green Dragon was going next: Belize. As I sat up from my **horizontal** position near the vent I saw that Dr. Science was also listening. His face had gone from its normal pale color to a shade of red and he glared at the secret door with great **fervor**. He must have known that behind that door was what he wanted more than anything else in the world and he'd have to prepare Little Lola and Asha Bloom for a quick trip to Belize **lest** he lose The Green Dragon for good.

Fill in the Blank

Choose the word that best completes each of the following sentences.

1. Wilbur thought that he was the _____ of the family even though he was the youngest son.

    a. patriarch

    b. boss

    c. founding member

    d. clown

2. Samantha often grew very _____ after her gymnastics class.

    a. sad

    b. silly

    c. weary

    d. funky

3. Jane considered herself the smartest in her class because she was often called _____.

   a. angry

   b. pensive

   c. defensive

   d. wistful

4. When you're in a sad mood it isn't wise to _____; try singing a song to cheer yourself up.

   a. wallow

   b. pout

   c. throw a tantrum

   d. take a nap

5. It is a crime to commit _____ in a court of law.

   a. silliness

   b. sulking

   c. suicide

   d. perjury

6. Russell was known for his _____ smile and charming attitude.

   a. invisible

   b. dirty

   c. vivacious

   d. silky

7. Jeremy often got bored in his Math class because his teacher was very _____.

   a. redundant

   b. quiet

   c. foolish

   d. creepy

8. Mrs. Pots hated to _____ her students, but sometimes she had to.

   a. laugh at

   b. karate chop

   c. frown at

   d. reprimand

9. Mandy's hair often looked _____
    because she didn't brush it in the morning
    before she went to school.

    a. stupid

    b. mangy

    c. beautiful

    d. sleepy

10. As Jonathan _____ into the quiet
    room he realized that his friends had decided
    to throw him a surprise birthday party.

    a. peered

    b. sat

    c. skipped

    d. fled

11. It is a tradition that a groom carries his bride
    over the _____ of their new home.

    a. roof

    b. fence

    c. lawn

    d. threshold

12. Owls are known to seek out mice as their
    _____.

    a. dinner

    b. prey

    c. friends

    d. students

13. A lot of people think that it is _____
    to have a coffee shop located on every corner.

    a. funny

    b. wise

    c. nice

    d. convenient

14. Michael's father is very _____ about
    his political ideas.

    a. staunch

    b. crazy

    c. boring

    d. selfish

15. Nobody likes to _____ with their friends.

    a. share

    b. quarrel

    c. cheat

    d. dance

QUIZ #13

Matching

Match each word on the left to a word with the similar meaning on the right.

1.	allure	a.	imitate
2.	obscure	b.	serious
3.	mimic	c.	declare
4.	faction	d.	murder
5.	listless	e.	sunset
6.	baffle	f.	tired
7.	earnest	g.	attraction
8.	cliché	h.	group
9.	assert	i.	hippie
10.	didactic	j.	commonplace
11.	hone	k.	rush
12.	manslaughter	l.	instructive
13.	bohemian	m.	practice
14.	dusk	n.	confuse
15.	expedite	o.	unclear

Matching

Match each word on the left to a word with the similar meaning on the right.

1.	awkward	a.	prevent
2.	cult	b.	maze
3.	genocide	c.	hunger
4.	labyrinth	d.	happy
5.	content	e.	gather
6.	abrupt	f.	not strong
7.	deter	g.	clumsy
8.	extraordinary	h.	play
9.	condone	i.	believers
10.	flimsy	j.	passion
11.	ebb	k.	melt
12.	dabble	l.	extermination
13.	fervor	m.	accept
14.	compile	n.	impolite
15.	famine	o.	amazing

True or False

Decide whether the following statements are True or False about Chapter 1. If the statement is true, write a "T" next to it. If the statement is false, write an "F" next to it.

1. Fredrick P. Honeycutt was the first known person to excavate The Green Dragon.
2. Guru Doug and Linda's abode does not have a golden toilet.
3. Diane, the strangely dressed woman, thinks that pasta is not bland without cheese.
4. The Cat thinks that red velvet curtains with orange polka-dots are vulgar.
5. Whenever Little Lola speaks about The Cat Dr. Science has some kind of retort.
6. Guru Doug is omnipotent.
7. There are several myths surrounding the powers of The Green Dragon.
8. Asha Bloom has a dogmatic personality.
9. The Green Dragon was never meant to be an heirloom to Honeycutt's daughter.
10. Guru Doug and Linda live in a very modest house.
11. Many people gyrate their hips at Guru Doug's daily disco.
12. Linda has a lot of anxiety about The Green Dragon.

13. It is ironic that Guru Doug was using The Green Dragon to gain wealth when he had to give it away to Sidney Whitehall to pay off a debt.

14. Dr. Science frequently kowtows to Asha Bloom's wishes.

15. Guru Doug inherited The Green Dragon from the Elephant King.

QUIZ #16

Relationships

Decide what type of relationship the words below have to each other. If the words have similar meanings, write "S" next to the pair of words. If they have different or opposite meanings, write "O" next to the words.

1. bane :: misery
2. eradicate :: destroy
3. finesse :: clumsiness
4. mentor :: teacher
5. contempt :: love
6. curt :: nice
7. dubious :: positive
8. lest :: for fear that
9. exodus :: arrival
10. humble :: grand

11. fraud :: fake
12. eccentric :: normal
13. forgo :: go without
14. literal :: actual
15. fatigue :: energy

CHAPTER 4
You Better Belize It

I'm sure it's hard to **comprehend** why anyone would take a cruise ship to Belize rather than just getting on a plane and flying there, but I had my reasons and they were good ones. As I left Guru Doug's with the knowledge that he had been **blackmailed** and threatened by Sidney Whitehall, I knew that I had to give up my quest following Dr. Science, Ms. Bloom, and Little Lola in exchange for staying on track with the man who now had The Green Dragon. And the man who now had The Green Dragon was taking a cruise ship to Belize instead of an airplane.

Although they're slower, cruise ships are far more comfortable than airplanes: There's always plenty of leg room, and if you're bored you can go to the buffet or casino. I wasn't on board to gamble, though. I was on board to follow Jagger Powerforce, the man who had **relieved** Guru Doug of The Green Dragon and was taking it to Sidney Whitehall. This was certainly no surprise to me as Jagger Powerforce has been a known **accomplice** of Mr. Whitehall's for years.

Sidney Whitehall and Jagger were a perfect criminal match. What Mr. Whitehall lacked in muscle Jagger Powerforce provided. And Sidney made up for what Jagger Powerforce lacked in the smarts department. The two of them were classic **caricatures** of people who devoted their lives to organized crime: one being the brains, the other the **brawn**. The only thing that complicated this relationship was that both of them had at one time or another dated Asha Bloom. If my spy skills have taught me anything over the years it's that you should never get involved in a love triangle, but I had a gut feeling that this was going to be **unavoidable**. And I was right.

Just as I was settling into my ship cabin I heard an all too familiar voice. It was Asha Bloom's. "Well, what did he look like, Dr. Science?"

"He was all muscle and no brain," Dr. Science said. "Why does it even matter? He's the one who has The Green Dragon and we have to get it from him before he gets it to Sidney Whitehall."

"Sidney Whitehall?" Asha and Little Lola said in **unison**.

"Yes, Sidney Whitehall," replied Dr. Science. "Now let's go to the buffet, I'm bored and not a little bit hungry."

It was now clear I wasn't the only one on board looking for Jagger Powerforce. Dr. Science, Asha Bloom, and Little Lola had also made it aboard and were presumably going to make trouble in Belize. But for now, they were headed where I was headed—the buffet.

OOOOOOOOOOOO

I really do love buffets, there are so many wonderful foods to try. You can make yourself a salad, have some hot potato soup, enjoy some king crab legs, **devour** a piece of prime rib, and then take a trip to the dessert bar and get a big piece of peach cobbler with a little piece of mint leaf as a **garnish**. It's a perfectly **ideal** way to spend an afternoon, especially if you're on a cruise ship. Fortunately, going to the buffet **coincided** with spying on the **exponential** number of criminals on board. Not only did I have to keep an eye out for Jagger Power-force, but also Dr. Science, Lola, and Asha as well. This time, however, I wanted to stay hidden. If they caught sight of me they'd know I was up to something and I certainly didn't want to **arouse** their suspicions, so instead of sitting in the middle of the grand dining hall, I sat near the kitchen and tried to observe everyone's behavior.

Asha Bloom came to the dining hall dressed in a green ball gown. She'd done her hair and was obviously looking to catch someone's attention, most likely Jagger's. But even without the fancy clothes it would have been impossible for anyone to miss her with those ridiculous sunglasses she insisted on wearing at all times.

Little Lola hadn't changed a thing about her appearance. She was still wearing that same old ball cap. She was, however, looking around the room nervously. Asha had most likely told her to look out for Jagger Powerforce.

Dr. Science was the only one to appear normal. Wearing his **durable** white lab coat he sat at one of the round dining tables and looked as if he were **contemplating** something important. He probably had his mind on Jagger Powerforce, too, but for different reasons.

Observing people's behavior can be very helpful when you're trying to spy on them. When they appear nervous, you know they're up to something, like Asha and Lola. And when they appear calm, you know they're planning something, like Dr. Science. As much as looking on is helpful, it's clearly better if you can use both your eyes and your ears. I knew that if I stayed near the kitchen door I'd never get the information I needed so

I decided to **instigate** a new plan: I'd dress up like one of the waiters in order to get closer.

I approached Asha, Lola, and Dr. Science's table wearing a pair of purple pants, a white dress shirt, and a gold bowtie. I looked just like all the other waiters. "What would you like to drink?" I asked them in my best imitation waiter voice.

"I'll have a glass of your best champagne," Asha requested.

"And I'd like an orange soda," Little Lola added.

"And for you, Sir?" I asked Dr. Science.

"It isn't 'Sir,' it's Doctor. I'll have a glass of sparkling mineral water with a slice of lime and no ice. I'm allergic to ice."

"That's a strange allergy," I commented.

"Nobody asked you," Dr. Science said rudely, making me realize why it's much better to be a spy than a waiter. People can be so demanding and mean.

I left to get their beverages and when I returned I heard Asha say, "Lola, look, there he is." I set down each beverage and then quickly looked to my right. There he was, the man who had The Green Dragon and Asha Bloom's ex-boyfriend, Jagger Powerforce.

I must admit that what I saw wasn't at all what I was expecting. Jagger Powerforce was quite possibly the strongest looking person I'd ever seen in life. Not only did he have muscles growing out of other muscles, but he had four arms **protruding** from a specially tailored vest instead of two.

"Oh wow, he's even more muscular than I thought," Little Lola said to Asha.

"I know. He has a **hearty** appetite for two things: going to the gym and eating king crab legs. Now, stop looking at him, Lola. I want him to notice me first," Asha said. And notice her he did. After Jagger Power-force filled up a plate with king crab legs her came over to the criminal's table while Dr. Science looked on in horror.

"Well, well, well, if it isn't Asha Bloom," Jagger said in an intimidating voice.

"My goodness, Jagger Powerforce, what on earth are you doing here?" Asha exclaimed, pretending that she didn't already know he was on board the ship.

Jagger began to **recount** some made up story about how he had injured himself playing a **hostile** game of rugby. "...after all that, I really needed to **rehabilitate** my muscles, so I decided to take a vacation to Belize."

During his explanation Dr. Science glared at Jagger Powerforce knowing full well that he was lying and that the real reason he was headed to Belize was to deliver The Green Dragon to Sidney Whitehall. Dr. Science also found himself completely confused and full of **envy** about the nature of Asha's relationship with Jag-ger Powerforce. As Asha was busy chatting to Jagger

Powerforce the only person he could turn to was Little Lola who was ignoring both of them and enjoying her orange soda.

"Lola, Lola, stop that, will you? Stop slurping up that disgusting drink and pay attention to me," Dr. Science whispered quietly while I polished some silverware.

"But it tastes good," Lola argued.

"What is going on here, Lola? How do those two know each other?" Dr. Science asked.

"Um, I think they used to go out with each other," Lola answered and continued to suck down the rest of her orange soda.

"Go out with each other?"

"Yeah," Lola said, "they went out on dates with each other."

The longer he stayed at the table the more troubled Dr. Science began to look. Finally, after staring at Asha and Jagger Powerforce for five whole minutes he stood up and excused himself. "You'll have to forgive me," he said, "I'm feeling a little **squeamish**. I think I'll go back to the cabin and lie down for the rest of the evening."

"Suit yourself, Dr. Science," Lola said. Asha said nothing as she was so consumed with Jagger she didn't even notice Dr. Science leaving.

This situation presented a problem. I couldn't decide who was more important to spy on. Was it better to follow Dr. Science back to his cabin and see if he was plotting anything or to stay in the dining hall to see if Jagger Powerforce revealed anything about The Green Dragon? Just as I was trying to make up my mind Little

Lola snapped her fingers at me and said, "Hey, I'm out of orange soda!" It was then clear to me that I should stop this **charade** as a waiter and follow Dr. Science back to his cabin or it was going to be a very, very long trip to Belize.

I followed Dr. Science to the casino where he sat at a colorful slot machine. He put coin after coin into the machine, pulled the shiny lever, and lost each time. He looked completely miserable. I knew he wouldn't be going anywhere, so I decided to go ahead of him to see if there were any clues near his cabin. It was very lucky that I made that decision because when I arrived at his cabin door there was a note taped to it. I grabbed the note and stared at the handwriting. It was practically **illegible**, but I managed to make out what it said:

> Dr. Science,
> Don't worry. I know what I'm doing.
>   Sincerely,
>   Asha Bloom

Obviously, Asha was up to something and that something involved Jagger Powerforce.

Before I even had to consider what Asha was up to I saw Dr. Science coming down the hall. I quickly taped the note back to the door, ducked back into my cabin, and left the door a little **ajar** so I could see Dr. Science's reaction to the note. It appeared that he had just as hard a time as I did trying to figure out what the handwriting said, but eventually I saw a smile come over his face and a look in his eyes that meant he was up to something.

The **duration** of the cruise to Belize appeared to any onlooker as normal, but to me it was very odd. Dr. Science, Asha Bloom, and Little Lola all kept their distance from one another. Asha Bloom flirted with Jagger Powerforce, Jagger Powerforce lifted weights in the gym on board, Dr. Science stayed in his cabin, Little Lola sunbathed on one of the deck chairs while drinking orange soda, and I waited for them to run into each other. I was expecting some sort of **debacle** to take place on board the ship, but absolutely nothing happened until the ship docked.

○○○○○○○○○○○

It was obvious that something had been planned on the ship because as soon as we set foot on dry land a big, black limousine pulled up to the dock. A very short man got out of the back seat followed by a very tall blonde. It was Sidney Whitehall and his girlfriend, Candie Cottonshank. I must admit that they were dressed with quite a bit of **panache**. Sidney was wearing a very small tuxedo and a pair of fancy sunglasses much like Asha Bloom's. Ms. Cottonshank's red **scanty** dress was quite short and didn't leave much to the imagination. Her heels were quite high and she was wearing what appeared to be more lipstick than clothing. I could tell that Asha Bloom wasn't very happy to see Ms. Cottonshank get out of the limousine with Sidney Whitehall and, to be honest with you, neither was I.

Jagger Powerforce immediately approached Sidney Whitehall and handed over what was obviously The

Green Dragon. "Put this in your purse, Sugar," Sidney said to Candie Cottonshank as he handed her the emerald. "You've finally done a good job, Jagger. I think you're actually starting to work well as my personal **liaison**." What happened next was a complete surprise. Jagger Powerforce let out a high-pitched, **boisterous** laugh and grabbed both Dr. Science and me while Sidney pulled a gun out of his fancy black tuxedo and pointed it at Asha and Little Lola.

"Hey, put me down you oaf!" Dr. Science yelled while Little Lola let out a little scream.

"Is this really necessary, Sidney?" Asha asked calmly.

"Of course it's necessary, Asha Bloom. I've known for ages now that you and your cohorts have been longing to get your hands on The Green Dragon, and I am not about to let that happen."

"OK, OK, maybe you're right, Sidney, but what if we **forfeit** our efforts in exchange for you letting us go?" Asha asked.

"No way, no how, Ms. Bloom. We're going to do this my way. Now you and your buddies and your pet kitty are going to go for a ride in my limousine," Sidney said as he forced Little Lola and Asha into the back of his car.

"But where are we going?" Little Lola asked in a frightened voice.

"To a secret **locale**. That's all you need to know," Candie Cottonshank said.

"That's right, we're going to my top secret **oasis,** and when we get there you're going to **disclose** to me the mysteries of The Green Dragon," Sidney Whitehall added as the rest of us were shoved into the back of the limousine. This was a **dilemma** for all of us. I'm quite certain that at this point none of us really knew how to unlock the powers of The Green Dragon, but before we could **articulate** our lack of knowledge the limousine took a sharp turn and started to **veer** away from the pier.

OOOOOOOOOOOO

I tried to keep a clear head in order to **navigate** precisely the location of Sidney Whitehall's headquarters, but found it rather difficult as Little Lola was holding me tightly and scratching behind my ears. "It's OK, little kitty," she said, "I'm so glad you found us. I was so worried about you. I didn't want to leave you all alone in that strange house in Italy with Guru Doug."

"Will you shut up?" Candie Cottonshank interrupted. "We don't care about your stupid cat."

While Little Lola ignored Ms. Cottonshank's rude remarks and remained completely **engrossed** in petting me, Dr. Science stared at Asha and wondered how they could have gotten themselves into this mess. I later found out that their **initial** plan was to have Asha flirt with Jagger Powerforce until she could convince him that it was more important for her to have The Green Dragon than it was for Sidney Whitehall to have it. She went as far as to **tantalize** him with new work-out pants and special protein shakes after his daily gym routine, but it was to no **avail**, he wouldn't give into what she wanted.

When we arrived at Sidney Whitehall's headquarters it appeared as if we had come to some sort of **mirage**. There was a big golden gate with the initials "SW" set right in the middle, and when the limousine drove up the gate opened and the "SW' separated. Inside the gates, there were the remains of what must have been ancient dwellings. I believe these dwellings were the ruins of and ancient people called the Mayans, who used to **inhabit** them. We were driven to one of the larger dwellings and then forced out of the car by Jagger Powerforce. Once inside Sidney Whitehall said, "Jagger, tie them all up and put them near the stairwell. And be quick about it. I don't want you **loafing** around today—Candie and I have an appointment to go deep-sea fishing." Jagger **diligently** picked each of us up in one of his powerful arms and carried us towards the stairwell. It wasn't the safest of spots to be. When you looked down there was a huge pile of **debris**. I, for one, was absolutely certain that I didn't want to fall down to the bottom of that stairwell because I knew at the end of the fall my bones would be in some kind of **melee**. There wasn't much time to worry about that, however, because Jagger Powerforce **lurched** forward, piling us all on top of each other. One by one he tied us up. Asha Bloom pouted and tried to get Jagger to untie her. Little Lola kicked and squirmed and tried to **gouge** him in the eye. Dr. Science acted **indifferent** to being tied up. And I, having been tied up many times before, held out my wrists in such a fashion that I'd be able to easily untie myself later on. "Make sure the ropes are good and tight, Jagger. I don't want anyone escaping and stealing The Green Dragon," Sidney Whitehall said as he went into a different room with Candie Cottonshank.

When Sidney and Candie returned they were dressed to fish, complete with poles and hooks. Mr. Whitehall even had a little tackle box which he came over to show us. "I'm sure you'd all love to see what's inside this little box, wouldn't you?" he asked as he opened it. Instead of worms and fish bait, which are normally found in most tackle boxes, there were hundreds of little emeralds. "Fish really respond well to shiny things like emeralds. I can only imagine how everyone will respond when I unlock the mysterious powers of The Green Dragon," he said with the **idiom** of a criminal mastermind. We were all stunned by this tackle box full of treasure. Our mouths widened to a **gape** when confronted by the sight of all those sparkling emeralds.

"Oh, Sid, you're so funny and smart and handsome," Candie Cottonshank **extolled** while Asha Bloom rolled her eyes behind her sunglasses. "There's no telling what we'll do with that giant green rock, is there?" She smiled, put her purse on a chair near the door, and grabbed her fishing pole.

"No, there's not, my dear," Sidney said as he closed his tackle box and headed for the door. "You guys have fun being tied up while we enjoy our **siesta** deep-sea fishing. Come on, Jagger, let's go. We don't want to miss the boat." And with that the three new **foes** left the dwelling for a deep-sea fishing excursion.

OOOOOOOOOOOO

"That was some plan, Asha," Dr. Science said **flippantly** as he tried to get his wrists free from the ropes.

"Don't be such a **cynic**. It would have worked if you hadn't have stomped off that first night on the ship," Asha replied.

"Do you have anymore brilliant ideas? Perhaps you can flirt with these ropes and they'll magically let us free," Dr. Science grumbled. "Lola, what on earth are you doing?" he added.

"Be quiet, Dr. Science. I'm trying to **meditate**," Lola responded in a calm voice.

"Why are you doing that? We're in a bit of an emergency. I don't want to spend the rest of my life tied up next to this dirty stairwell hoping Sidney Whitehall and his dumb girlfriend drown in the ocean while they're deep-sea fishing," Asha said.

"Guru Doug told me that if you put yourself in a calm frame of mind and concentrate on what you want most that you will be **alleviated** of all your troubles and you'll have whatever you wish," Lola answered while breathing very deeply.

"What a bunch of hooey," Dr. Science said. "There's no scientific evidence to prove that. None at all."

"Yeah," added Asha Bloom, "look where Guru Doug is now, stuck in Calcata without his precious Green Dragon." Just then we all felt a strange **gust** of wind blow through the open window. "Oh great, now the wind is going to mess up my hair," Asha continued. "Lola, why don't you concentrate on keeping the wind blowing the other way instead?"

Lola ignored both Dr. Science and Asha's **pessimism** and continued to sit cross-legged with her eyes closed. The wind, it seemed, was gaining **momentum** and started blowing even harder. Suddenly, Little Lola burst free of her ropes and smiled. "Tada!" she shouted as if she had performed some great magic trick. I, too, had escaped my ropes, but instead of meditating, I used good old-fashioned spy knowledge.

With Dr. Science and Asha Bloom still tied up I thought it would be wise of me to run over to Candie Cottonshank's purse and grab The Green Dragon, but before I could move an inch Lola picked me up and started petting me again. "There, there, little kitty," she said. "You're going to be all right. I won't let that mean man tie you up ever again."

"Will you stop fooling around with that cat and untie us," Dr. Science shouted. Instead of setting me down, Lola held me tight around the neck and untied both Asha Bloom and Dr. Science. It was a very uncomfortable situation. Not only was I being strangled, but The Green Dragon was only feet away in Candie Cottonshank's purse.

As soon as they'd been untied, Dr. Science and Asha started arguing again and Little Lola started scratching behind my ears. I did what any spy disguised as a cat would do in this sort of **adverse** situation, I purred and pointed my tail at Candie's purse hoping that Lola would realize that The Green Dragon was close by. My plan worked. While Asha told Dr. Science what an idiot he was and how he had "super-terrible fashion sense," Lola sneaked over and grabbed The Green Dragon.

"Look what I found," Lola shouted. Both Dr. Science and Asha looked over and smiled with greed. I tried to grab the emerald, but was unsuccessful. Little Lola was still holding me tightly around my neck like she would hold a loved stuffed animal.

"Give that to me," Dr. Science demanded as he rushed over toward Lola.

Lola refused and put The Green Dragon underneath her cap. And then, all of the sudden, Sidney Whitehall, Candie Cottonshank, and Jagger Powerforce burst in yelling something about a **monsoon**.

"It's raining tigers and bears out there," Candie Cottonshank cried as she rushed into the dwelling soaking wet.

"I think you mean bats and frogs," Jagger Powerforce **contradicted**.

"No, you idiots, it's cats and dogs," Sidney Whitehall said, correcting them both while Ms. Cottonshank looked for her purse.

"Sidney, Sidney, my purse," she said trying to get his full attention.

"Shut up, will you? I want to get out of these wet things before I catch some kind of nasty disease," Sidney said **basely**.

"But Sidney, The Green Dragon, it's gone!" she finally yelled.

Sidney Whitehall looked around the dwelling and was shocked to see that we had all somehow broken free of our ropes. It made him very angry. "Jagger, don't just sit there looking like a **pacifist**! Get them," he yelled as Jagger Powerforce tried to grab us each in one of his arms. Dr. Science had already come up with a plan to escape, however.

As the storm blew outside, Dr. Science handed Little Lola one of her favorite things, a piece of bubble gum. But this wasn't your typical piece of gum. It was a high **caliber** chewing gum that he himself had invented so that when it was blown into a bubble it created a very strong balloon. "Blow a bubble, Lola. Blow the biggest bubble you can," he told her as we all gathered around her. As she blew the bubble she started to float. One by one we all grabbed on to Little Lola. Jagger Powerforce looked on with complete confusion. Sidney Whitehall was yelling about the **upheaval** and trouble we were causing. And Ms. Candie Cottonshank was putting on more lipstick.

Finally, the bubble grew big enough to carry us all. We placed ourselves in the path of the storm and were carried away up into the **ozone layer**, but before I could **revel** in the knowledge that The Green Dragon had been stolen from Sidney Whitehall, I first had to accept that it was Little Lola who had stolen it. And despite her recent stubbornness to keep the beautiful emerald under her precious cap, I knew eventually she'd give it up to Dr. Science.

QUIZ #17

Relationships

Decide what type of relationship the words below have to each other. If the words have similar meanings, write "S" next to the pair of words. If they have different or opposite meanings, write "O" next to the words.

1. ajar :: closed
2. siesta :: nap
3. revel :: celebrate
4. momentum :: slow down
5. monsoon :: storm
6. extol :: make fun of
7. dilemma :: problem
8. melee :: tidy
9. foe :: friend
10. recount :: retell
11. unison :: alone
12. hostile :: pleasant
13. durable :: sturdy
14. gouge :: prick
15. base :: vulgar

Relationships

Decide what type of relationship the words below have to each other. If the words have similar meanings, write "S" next to the pair of words. If they have different or opposite meanings, write "O" next to the words.

1. pacifist :: peaceable
2. forfeit :: abandon
3. gape :: ignore
4. garnish :: leave plain
5. oasis :: retreat
6. devour :: consume
7. adverse :: advantageous
8. scanty :: plentiful
9. accomplice :: enemy
10. meditate :: contemplate
11. exponential :: decreasing
12. envy :: jealousy
13. flippant :: mannered
14. brawn :: scrawny
15. ideal :: perfect

Fill in the Blank

Choose the word that best completes each of the following sentences.

1. When Harry saw that he had to dissect a frog he started to feel a little _____.

   a. silly

   b. angry

   c. squeamish

   d. fatigued

2. Mark's birthday _____ with his uncle's birthday.

   a. coincides

   b. appears

   c. happens

   d. reflects

3. The film shoot had to stop early because it had started raining on their desired _____.

   a. camera

   b. movie star

   c. lunch

   d. locale

4. When the principal announced that school would be closed for the _____ of the school year all the students cheered.

   a. duration

   b. discontinuation

   c. whole

   d. passing

5. Being from a foreign country, Nancy's speech was full of different _____.

   a. jokes

   b. sounds

   c. idioms

   d. nouns

6. Sean always won in his debate class because he knew how to _____ an argument very well.

   a. spell out

   b. describe

   c. write

   d. articulate

7. Mrs. Smith's car _____ just in time to not hit the dear in the road.

   a. fell

   b. veered

   c. slid

   d. sped

8. Many top environmentalists say that if we don't start recycling more often then we will completely ruin the _____.

   a. supermarket

   b. airport safety

   c. government

   d. Ozone Layer

9. When Charles lost his way he had to backtrack where he'd been in order to _____ his way home.

   a. navigate

   b. consider

   c. discover

   d. run

10. Walter could not _____ how a giraffe from the zoo had made it into his backyard.

    a. picture

    b. believe

    c. deliver

    d. comprehend

11. Sylvia was almost blown completely over by a sudden, strong _____ of wind.

    a. gust

    b. rush

    c. burst

    d. slap

12. Mary's friends often called her a _____ because she never believed a word anyone said.

    a. bore

    b. cynic

    c. liar

    d. drunk

13. When handing in your homework it is very important that your handwriting is not _____ because you might get a bad grade if the teacher can't read it.

    a. readable

    b. pretty

    c. illegible

    d. neat

14. Emily sprained her ankle during soccer practice and was sent home to _____.

    a. watch tv

    b. rehabilitate

    c. injure

    d. prepare

15. Aidan was known for all the funny _____ he drew of his classmates.

    a. caricatures

    b. comic books

    c. descriptions

    d. faces

16. Mary knew getting a bad grade on her spelling test was _____ because she hadn't studied all week.

    a. acceptable

    b. exciting

    c. escapable

    d. unavoidable

Matching

Match each word on the left to a word with the similar meaning on the right.

1. avail
2. contradict
3. debacle
4. arouse
5. alleviate
6. lurch
7. blackmail
8. pessimism
9. tantalize
10. loaf
11. indifferent
12. panache
13. debris
14. instigate

a. jerk
b. tease
c. relieve
d. rubble
e. dilly dally
f. bribe
g. oppose
h. uninterested
i. excite
j. available
k. activate
l. style
m. hopelessness
n. disaster

Matching

Match each word on the left to a word with the similar meaning on the right.

1. boisterous	a. quality
2. relieve	b. disorder
3. contemplate	c. expose
4. mirage	d. captivate
5. protrude	e. hallucination
6. diligent	f. beginning
7. caliber	g. rowdy
8. charade	h. reside
9. engross	i. persevering
10. upheaval	j. think
11. initial	k. energetic
12. liaison	l. comforting
13. inhabit	m. pretend
14. hearty	n. contact
15. disclose	o. stick out

CHAPTER 5
The Honeycutt connection

I've got to tell you that holding tightly to Dr. Science's leg while floating through the air and hoping that a big bubble doesn't pop isn't really my idea of a fun time. Not only was I hoping that the bubble wouldn't pop, but I was also concerned that one of us might slip and become the first **casualty**. I tried to keep an attitude of **optimism,** yet I was worried that if one of us fell, particularly me, I'd end up **unconscious** in some strange place and The Green Dragon would be out of my reach.

Thankfully, that didn't happen and as the winds died down we gently glided to the ground where we were set down next to a natural **levee** of some sort. Such **ecstasy**, such joy, I'd never felt so happy to be alive until I realized I was now stuck with a rather **cumbersome** bunch of criminals who seemed to think that arguing was a sport. With much **disdain** I allowed myself to curl into the arms of Little Lola while she participated in yet another **spat** with Dr. Science and Asha Bloom.

"Lola, give me The Green Dragon," Dr. Science demanded immediately after he'd set foot on the ground.

"But it's mine," she argued. "I'm the one who stole it from Ms. Cottonshank."

"Lola, listen to me," Dr. Science continued, "if it weren't for me and my quick thinking you'd still be in Belize, but instead of being happy and healthy like you appear right now, you'd be either a **paraplegic** or a **corpse**."

"Oh yeah, well, you'd be a, you'd be a..." It was obvious that Little Lola was having trouble coming up with something to call Dr. Science, but that she wasn't going to give him what he wanted, so he tried a different approach.

"Lola, sweet, dear, Little Lola," he said "Let me help you. I can help you discover how to properly use The Green Dragon to its fullest potential. I'm a scientist, Lola, we know everything."

"Stop trying to **patronize** her, Dr. Science," Asha finally interrupted.

"Yeah, stop trying to do that thing that Asha said," Lola chimed in.

"Ladies, ladies, please," Dr. Science said knowing he was backing himself into a corner, "I'm only trying to help. Isn't that the reason you wanted me to come and help you with your little adventure in the first place? Didn't you come to me, Ms. Bloom asking if I could help you steal The Green Dragon, so that you could use it as a bargaining tool to steal more jewels? How can you do that if you don't know how to unlock its secrets?"

"I suppose you're right, Dr. Science," Asha said while Little Lola nodded in agreement.

"All right then instead of all this arguing we need to come up with a plan," Dr. Science said in a **resolute** manner. So, as the sun started to set, the four of us sat in a circle not knowing exactly where we were, but determined to **rectify** the unpleasant and rather **vulnerable** situation we'd gotten ourselves into. Dr. Science pulled a map out of his white lab coat, Asha tried to fix her hair, and Little Lola decided to **torment** me by pulling small pieces of bubblegum out of my furry disguise.

As Dr. Science remained **preoccupied** with his map, Asha and Lola got a little restless.

"How long are you planning on staring at that thing?" Asha asked in a **snide** tone of voice.

"As long as it takes to figure out where we are," he answered in a similar tone while Little Lola kept picking at my fur. I was sincerely starting to **lament** my decision to come with them when a very strange man approached us. He looked like a **nomad**. The soles of his sandals were worn bare, his clothing wasn't very clean, his beard was very long, and he had that scent of a traveler about him. There was something a little strange though, almost **supernatural** about the man. Although his beard was long and white, his eyes and face looked very young. His presence seemed like some kind of **omen**.

"Are you lost?" the man asked as he reached us.

Dr. Science, being the arrogant scientist that he was, replied, "Of course we're not lost. I'm just finding where we are on the map is all."

"What do you mean we're not lost?" Asha Bloom **scoffed**. "We're completely lost and you've been looking at that map for hours."

"Asha, there's no need to go telling our business to complete strangers," Dr. Science said.

"But maybe he can help us, Dr. Science," Little Lola added while she held me tightly in her lap.

"I can help you, certainly I can, but only if you want help. That is the key," the man said mysteriously.

"Well, I for one, would like some help. I'm sick of sitting around in all this **atrocious** nature," Asha said.

"Then help you shall have," the man said. "You only have to ask for it."

"Tell us where we are, so we can get out of here," Asha said none too politely.

"Follow me," the man said.

"Follow you? Why would we follow you? That will only get us more lost," Dr. Science tried to reason.

"Before you can find your way, you must first become lost," the man said smiling. "That is the best trick of all."

"What are you on about?" Asha said looking the man up and down. "And where did you get those ugly sandals?"

It seemed that the only person who was willing to try anything was Little Lola and since she was the one with The Green Dragon under her cap the rest had to follow her. "I don't care what the two of you do, but I'm going with him. He might have some food and water and I'm starving," Lola said as she took out her shoelace and tied it around my neck like a little leash. I hated to agree with her, but she was right, so I meowed as best I could and got up to follow her and the strange man. Dr. Science and Asha Bloom reluctantly came along.

The man led us far away from where we had been. It felt as if we were walking on **hallowed** ground or perhaps we were going to meet some kind of **grave** consequences as soon as we got to wherever we were going. And to make matters worse, no one was talking. At that point in time, I actually wished to hear Dr. Science and Asha Bloom arguing about something stupid, but they remained quiet. The situation felt incredibly **precarious**.

After what seemed like miles—anything can seem like miles if you're attached to a shoelace as a **makeshift** leash—the strange man with the beard told us to stop and close our eyes. "We have arrived," the man said quietly. "You must close your eyes." Lola immediately closed her eyes while both Dr. Science and Asha rolled theirs before closing them and I kept mine slightly open. The man clapped his hands together three times in a strange rhythm and suddenly a mansion appeared. "Here we are. This is my house." All of us stared on in wonder. How could a man dressed like a **pauper** be the owner of such a huge house? The answers awaited us inside.

○○○○○○○○○○○

The man took us inside the carved, wooden doors and led us into a magnificent entry way. The floors were made of marble and a very large staircase presented itself to us upon entering. It made Guru Doug's house **pale** in comparison. There were priceless works of heart hanging from the walls that distracted Dr. Science and a gold mirror that took up Asha's attention. I remained close to Little Lola having no other real choice in the matter. As she looked up at the ceiling and yawned the strange man with the beard observed, "Oh, yes, you all must be very tired after your journey. Let me show you to your rooms." He snapped his fingers and the staircase started to move up like an escalator. All of us stepped onto it wondering what would happen next.

Asha Bloom was shown to her room first. Even I was impressed with how luxurious it was. The bed was made of silver and rubies and there were mirrors all around making it appear as if the room never ended. Of course, Asha was fond of all the mirrors as it allowed her to see her reflection constantly.

Next was Dr. Science. His room looked just like a science lab. There were bottles of strange elements gathering dust on shelves and lots of little glass beakers and measuring instruments on a large table in the middle of the room. There was a giant globe near a big window and rows and rows of thick books lined two of the walls. The bed was shaped like a space ship which made Dr. Science smile a little despite himself.

Finally, we went to Little Lola's room which looked like a beach town. There was a wave pool in one corner where she could pick up a surf board and practice her surfing. There was a hot dog stand that gave you hot dogs, cotton candy, popcorn, and Lola's favorite, unlimited gallons of orange soda. There was a sandy beach with palm trees. And for a bed there was a giant hammock with lots and lots of pillows. Just as I was wondering where I was going to sleep, a little hammock appeared near Lola's. I thought my eyes were playing a trick on me as I hadn't seen the hammock when we first entered the room, but perhaps it was there all along. It's hard to say.

As we all got comfortable in our new rooms we heard a loud bell ring throughout the house and a soothing voice call out, "Dinner will be served in ten minutes in the dining hall."

Ten minutes later all of us were seated at a long wooden table wondering where on earth we were. Before we could ask any questions, our host, the strange man with the beard **emerged** from a hidden door with a little man dressed in a suit and funny top hat. He was holding what appeared to be some kind of magic wand.

"I do hope you all find your **accommodations satisfactory**," the strange man with the beard said. All of us agreed that they were beyond comfortable. "I'm very glad to hear it," the man with the beard said and snapped his fingers. With that, the other little man in the top hat brought out the most delicious looking food I'd ever seen. It was even better than the endless supply of king crab legs on the cruise ship. Our appetites were **insatiable** and we ate for what seemed like hours before any of us were full.

As our stomachs were finally **subdued** from their hunger, the man with the beard introduced his friend in the top hat. "This is Mr. Otto Pearlbutton. If you need anything during your stay, anything at all, just ask him and he will give it to you." Asha smiled at this knowledge while Little Lola and Dr. Science nodded happily. I, on the other hand, looked on in disbelief. Something wasn't right. "Now, if you have any questions, please feel free to ask me."

Dr. Science finally came out of his satisfied reverie and asked the man who he was. "It's very, uh, kind of you to let us stay here in your mansion, but, uh, we were, uh, just wondering who you were."

A large smile came across the strange man with a beard's face and with a wave of his hand he answered with a lot of **gusto**, "I am none other than Klaus Von Bonbon, the famous illusionist!"

OOOOOOOOOOOO

I'm not sure if you know any illusionists, but if you do, I'm sure you know that their **nocturnal** habits are rather odd. When dinner was over and the dishes some- how magically disappeared we were taken into a large sitting room with a warm fire. Klaus Von Bonbon sat down on the floor, his legs stretched out **perpendicular** at first, and then crossed and then stretched out again.

"Why do you keep squirming around like that?" Dr. Science finally asked him.

"It is not squirming, Doctor, it's stretching—surely you've heard of it," Klaus answered.

"Oh, all right, why do you keep stretching then?" Dr. Science asked again a little annoyed.

"No other reason than I like to have a good stretch after dinner," Von Bonbon answered.

"Well, that's kind of **insipid** isn't it? I mean, I was rather hoping to be amazed by some **hoax** or something," Asha blurted out, at which point the funny little man with the wand, Otto Pearlbutton, entered the sitting room and handed Klaus a little piece of string.

"Here you are, Master Von Bonbon. Here is what you asked for," Pearlbutton said.

Klaus thanked Otto and then asked Asha, "You want to see a trick then do you?"

"Yes, I'd love to see a trick," Asha said.

"Me too, me too. I want to see one," added Little Lola.

Klaus Von Bonbon stood up and stretched out his back and then his arms and returned to his regular sitting position near the fire with his legs crossed. He then tied the little piece of string that Otto Pearlbutton brought to him around his beard. We all sat watching anxiously for something to happen and, just as we were about to give up on Von Bonbon, Little Lola noticed that his beard was turning green. It happened slowly at first but the longer we watched Klaus Von Bonbon's beard began to **mutate** from one color to another. It started out green and then turned pink. From pink it went to peach and from peach it turned yellow. After yellow came a shade of blue and then purple. Finally, it turned orange and left us completely stunned. Little Lola and Asha started clapping their hands together as Dr. Science stared on in disbelief.

"I want to see another one," Lola shouted.

"I'm afraid it is late and I must be getting to bed. There will be plenty of time to see more tricks tomorrow," Von Bonbon said as he got up from the floor and stretched his back again. "I think it is all time for us to go to our rooms and get some much needed sleep. You wouldn't want to **deplete** me of all my energy, would you?"

"I guess not," Lola said as she stood and picked me up. "I am feeling a little tired."

"As am I," Dr. Science said.

"Yeah, I totally need my beauty sleep," Asha added. "You don't want to see me in the morning without it."

We all left the sitting room and stood on one of the stairs that suddenly started moving us up to the next level like an escalator. One by one, we went to our rooms while soothing music played all around us. "This music will **lull** you to sleep," Von Bonbon said as he entered his room waving goodnight to all of us.

As Little Lola climbed into her hammock I tried my hardest to stay awake and think about what had happened tonight, but the music was so incredibly soothing I was finding it very difficult. None of us knew where we were and it seemed like it no longer mattered to the other three. They appeared happy with staying in their luxurious rooms and watching little magic tricks. I had a deep feeling that something wasn't right. Not only did I feel that The Green Dragon was in danger, but so were we.

Staying in my little hammock for a good night's sleep was clearly not an option. I had to get to work. I simply had to see what Klaus Von Bonbon and Otto Pearlbutton were up to. Once I heard Little Lola start to snore I got up and sneaked out of the room. It was lucky that the music had stopped, otherwise I would have still been asleep in that fantastic room with the wave pool and endless supply of hot dogs. I searched for Von Bonbon's room, but couldn't seem to find it. I'd certainly seen him go into it. He waved goodnight to us from its doorway, but now, I couldn't find it for the life of me. Just when I thought all was lost and that I'd never find the door, Otto Pearlbutton appeared. My **innate** spy instinct was to follow him which led me straight to Klaus Von Bonbon.

OOOOOOOOOOOO

"What do you mean, Master Klaus? Are you telling me that they actually have The Green Dragon?" Otto asked as he quickly entered a large room. Carefully as a cat could, I sneaked in behind him. The room was incredible. The ceilings appeared to go all the way up to the sky and the walls were lined with rows and rows of boxes. Each of the boxes contained some sort of **radical** magic trick, at least that's what the labels led me to believe. As Pearlbutton sat down next to a **decoy** pair of legs belonging to a forgotten illusion, I hid behind an old sofa to better listen in on their conversation.

"Yes, Otto, I can feel it—I can feel the presence of The Green Dragon. It's especially strong when the younger one is around," Von Bonbon responded with a hint of **malice** in his voice.

"What are you going to do?" Otto asked a little nervously.

"Otto, you know that The Green Dragon is rightfully mine. Honeycutt was my **maternal** grandfather and he left The Green Dragon to my mother before she gave it to that Marcel woman. Obviously, I plan on taking back what belongs to me."

"Yes, but how, Master Klaus?" Otto asked.

"Otto, is my mansion not one of the most comfortable places in the world?"

"Yes, of course, Master Von Bonbon," Otto answered in a respectful and **servile** way.

"In fact, isn't it so comfortable that if one were staying here that they could get distracted by all the pleasures it offers?"

"Well, certainly it is comfortable and the pleasures are numerous," Otto responded again as if he were **beholden** to Von Bonbon.

"That is my answer, Otto. I will distract our guests with every possible pleasure. Any desire they have will be fulfilled and they will be so overwhelmed by my hospitality that I will be able to snatch away what is rightfully mine. I will take The Green Dragon," Von Bonbon said shrewdly.

"I see, Master Klaus. That is a brilliant plan."

"Yes, I know, Otto. We must first work on **exploiting** the smaller one, Little Lola. She is the most important of the three. Make sure that any wish of hers is your command. Treat her with the **dignity** and **prestige** of a princess, Otto."

"What about the other two?" Otto asked, worried that he'd have the same **obligation** to them as he now did to Little Lola.

"Once I get my hands on The Green Dragon I frankly wouldn't mind if the lot of them came down with **gout** or **ulcers**. In fact, I wouldn't care if you **decapitated** them, but until that time we've got to spoil them all **profusely**. I want the comforts of my mansion and my staff to **impair** their judgment. Is that understood?"

"Yes, Master Klaus, but—" Otto Pearlbutton began, but was interrupted by Von Bonbon.

"I'm sick of all your **rebuttals**, Otto. Now, make yourself useful and bring me a cup of tea," Klaus demanded like some sort of business **tycoon**.

Not wanting to upset Von Bonbon any longer Otto Pearlbutton left the room while I remained hidden. Once his servant had gone Klaus Von Bonbon picked up a very old leather book and turned to an **earmarked** page. He stared at the page for ages, mumbling things under his breath. Suddenly, Von Bonbon jumped out of his large chair twirled in a circle four times and again clapped his hands together like he had done earlier in the evening. It looked as if he were performing some kind of **pantomime** or playing a game of charades. Seconds after he'd finished his last clap a spiral staircase appeared out of thin air leading to a secret room. Von Bonbon left the book on a little table and climbed up the stairs. The second his foot fell on the last step he disappeared. I took advantage of his absence and immediately grabbed the book that he was reading.

Not wanting to be caught with the book if Klaus Von Bonbon returned from the staircase I took it back down to the sitting room where the once burning logs had turned into **embers**. The orange glow from the fireplace made the room appear a lot smaller than it actually was. It almost felt cozy as I sat next to the fireplace and let my eyes adjust to the light. I brushed a little dust from the cover of the book and then opened it. I could hardly believe my eyes when I got to the first page. The book was a diary that belonged to Frederick P. Honeycutt. If my instincts were as correct—as they usually were—the pages of the diary that I was holding contained all the secrets to unlocking The Green Dragon.

○○○○○○○○○○○○

If you've ever been really fascinated by a subject in a book then you know that sitting up all night and reading by the light of a dying fire isn't that crazy, which is exactly what I did with the diary. Honeycutt left a **prosaic** account of every single time he used The Green Dragon and what the effects were. There were stories and secrets about the first time he discovered how to use the enchanted emerald and the path he took from using it for mere entertainment purposes to much more **malignant** purposes later on in his life. The diary also revealed the secret to using the powerful emerald. There were a series of words that were to be said while rubbing the emerald with a gloved hand that would unlock its powers, and even though I learned the words, I will not share them. It would be far too dangerous.

One tale that really **captivated** my attention was an account of how he'd used The Green Dragon to **exhaust** the bank account of a **matriarch** from a well-known and **revered** political family. The woman was convinced by Honeycutt that The Green Dragon could help her son win his campaign for office and indeed it did. Whenever there was a speech to be given or questions to be answered by the **media**, Honeycutt would accompany the woman's son and unleash The Green Dragon in the midst of the crowd. No matter what **propaganda** the son was spreading, the crowds and journalists would agree with it. This account in Honeycutt's diary proves that with The Green Dragon large amounts of people could be fooled and perhaps even forced to do things against their will. In the wrong hands, The Green Dragon could be dangerous, even lethal. It could cause wars, famines, plagues, and worse. If it was capable of controlling peoples' behavior and thoughts, perhaps it was dangerous in even if in the right hands. After all, it's criminal not to let people have their own free will. Honeycutt admitted this freely in the later entries of his diary. It was almost as if the power of The Green

Dragon had taken hold of him, too, and in the end he was sorry for all that he'd done. He was sorry for the people he'd tricked and stolen from. He was sorry for taking peoples' right to choose away from them. The last entry in Honeycutt's diary says:

> I must **repent**. I have spent my adult life in the pursuit of harming people; I have taken away their ability to choose in both large and small doses. The power of The Green Dragon belongs in someone else's hands, someone who will not abuse it the way that I have. That is why I am leaving it to my dearest, Sarah. She will keep it safe.
>
> Sarah, my dear, if you read this, beware the power this emerald holds. Do not let it tempt you. It is beautiful, yes, but it is also evil. No one is **immune** to its power. Terrible things can happen if you let them.
>
> F.P. Honeycutt

It was obvious that Sarah Honeycutt had not read the diary or else she would have listened to her father's advice. She mistook The Green Dragon as something unimportant and gave it to Sophie Marcel and from there it got into the wrong hands: first, the Elephant King; next, Guru Doug; then, Sidney Whitehall; and finally, Little Lola. Although Little Lola clearly didn't know what The Green Dragon was capable of, others, like Dr. Science, Asha Bloom, and Klaus Von Bonbon did. I didn't know any of their **motives** for wanting The Green Dragon, but it was obvious to me that none of them were good.

After reading in the diary the accounts of Honeycutt's victims who had their ability to make choices and decisions taken away from them by The Green Dragon, I had an odd feeling of comfort from still having the ability to make a choice. As I looked out the window and noticed the sun coming up I found myself faced with a serious decision: I could either keep the diary and the secrets it held or I could destroy it. If I kept the diary I'd run the risk of it getting into the hands of Asha Bloom, or worse, Dr. Science, neither of whom knew the secret words that would unleash The Green Dragon's fearsome powers. If I destroyed the diary far fewer people would be able to use The Green Dragon as Honeycutt's secrets would no longer be available for anyone to read. I quickly read the note Honeycutt left for his daughter again and then repeated the words I'd learned to protect me against the powers of The Green Dragon, so I wouldn't forget them in case of an emergency. I decided that the best plan would be to quickly destroy the book, find out where in the world I was, get The Green Dragon from Little Lola, and destroy that as soon as I possibly could. Unfortunately, my plan didn't exactly work that way.

○○○○○○○○○○○○

Just as I had thrown Honeycutt's diary into the fireplace I heard footsteps coming towards the sitting room. The steps grew louder and quicker, quicker and louder as I blew on the little fire to make it burn faster. As the blaze slowly grew I heard the door burst open and saw Little Lola standing there with a panicked look on her face.

"Oh, kitty, there you are. I'd thought you'd run away. I was so worried." I ran over toward her and jumped on her. She mistook my romping as affection when really I was trying to knock the cap off her head in order to grab The Green Dragon and make a run for it. I misjudged her strength and instead of landing on top of her, I landed straight in her arms. She carried me out of the sitting room and I quickly looked in the direction of the fireplace. To my relief, Honeycutt's diary had caught fire and was letting off little green puffs of smoke up into the chimney.

Lola carried me into the dining room where we had all had dinner the previous night. It looked completely different this morning. The walls had turned bright yellow and instead of a grand dining table there was a smaller, more intimate table where Asha Bloom, Dr. Science, and Klaus Von Bonbon sat eating their breakfasts. Asha was eating a plate of delicious looking fruit, Dr. Science had a giant bowl of steaming oatmeal with honey, Klaus Von Bonbon was eating toast and a poached egg, and in front of Lola's chair was a giant stack of chocolate chip pancakes, a pile of bacon, and a big bottle of orange soda. "Look who I found sneaking around," she said as she sat down to her pancakes.

"What a naughty little kitty cat you've got there, Little Lola," Von Bonbon said in a **jovial** and obviously fake tone. "Otto, please bring Lola's cat some tuna fish." Now, I don't mind lightly seared slices of tuna fish served on a green salad with a nice dressing, or even a few skillfully cut pieces of sushi, but I absolutely hate canned tuna fish, which is exactly what Otto Pearlbutton put in front of me. Being disguised as a cat certainly has its downfalls from time to time and the assumption that all cats like to eat is canned tuna fish is one of them. I pushed it around the little red plate so it looked as if I'd eaten some and felt relieved when Lola sneaked me a piece of her bacon. Excluding the fact that she was a known criminal, I suppose Little Lola wasn't all that bad.

"I'm confused," Dr. Science said as Lola was feeding me scraps of bacon. "I did some research last night on the whereabouts of your mansion and I can't quite place the geographical location."

Klaus curled his lips into a smile and tried to hold back his **guile** as he answered, "My dear Dr. Science, my mansion isn't located on any maps. It's very well hidden."

"But how are we supposed to get out of here if we don't know where we are?" Asha asked suddenly interested.

"Precisely, my dear," Von Bonbon answered.

"What do you mean?" Dr. Science asked a little insistently.

Not wanting any of his guests to panic, Von Bonbon quickly answered, "Why would you want to leave this fabulous house when it contains every comfort and can fulfill any desire you have?"

"It is pretty fabulous," Asha admitted as Dr. Science gave her a dirty look across the table.

"I would like to know where we are," Dr. Science said firmly. Just then a silver and gold globe floated down from the ceiling and as Otto Pearlbutton cleared the breakfast dishes Klaus Von Bonbon began to explain.

"In the beginning of my career as an illusionist I found that I was often **persecuted** for my splendid tricks. Audiences weren't fond of being turned into monkeys and chickens. They didn't like it when I locked them up in cages and made them disappear in thin air. I found that instead of delighting them, my tricks and illusions just upset them. It got so bad in one town that my life was threatened. At this point, I thought it would be safer if I was the one who did the disappearing, so I built this mansion as a safe place for me to live and practice my craft."

"I understand the need for you to disappear," Dr. Science said. "I myself have found many to be unappreciative of my work as well."

"I appreciate it," Asha said.

Dr. Science's face hinted at a smile and, as breakfast turned into lunch, he explained his criminal career to

Klaus Von Bonbon. The two men started to bond over their similar pasts. Both felt that they were brilliant but misunderstood. Feeling that he'd finally found someone he could trust, Von Bonbon told Dr. Science where his mansion was located. "You see, I built it here, in the Pyrenees because it's quite remote and far from things, but not so far that I can't be in a city within a few hours. Not to mention the skiing is great."

"So, we're very close to France then," Dr. Science said.

"And Spain," Asha added.

Before any of us knew it, it was time for dinner. The walls changed from their sunny yellow color in the morning to a deep blue. The intimate table was replaced with a larger, more formal one, and Asha excused herself to dress for dinner. The rest of us remained there. When she returned, Asha was wearing a beautiful gown that made her look like a twinkling star set against the blue walls. Even Dr. Science was a bit stunned by the dress. As we all sat down to eat, Dr. Science kept trying to make eye contact with her, which she interpreted as flirting, but he was really just trying to get her attention. From the way he was responding to Von Bonbon's comments you could tell that he felt uncomfortable. You could tell that he wanted to leave. This wasn't the first time that Dr. Science and I had the same feeling, and it wouldn't be the last.

We were served dinner by Otto Pearlbutton, who had changed from his tuxedo and top hat to a footman's uniform and a powdered wig. He looked like some sort of servant from a French novel. Asha was served a grilled chicken and pear salad with walnuts and cran-berries. Dr. Science was given a big bowl of rabbit stew. Klaus Von Bonbon had scallops wrapped in bacon. And Little Lola was served a hot dog with an enormous plate of French fries. I was forced to push around an-other plateful of canned tuna. The dinner conversation was lively. Asha laughed at all Von Bonbon's jokes while Lola munched her French fries. Dr. Science kept kick-ing Asha under the table and missed once kicking me in the face on accident. It was obvious that he wanted to talk to her about something.

With our stomachs full, or rather, with their stom-achs full, Dr. Science, Asha Bloom, and Little Lola thought it best to go to bed early. Not wanting get in the way of their needs, Klaus Von Bonbon showed them all to their rooms again. Then he snapped his fingers and the same lullaby that had played the night before began to play. He then disappeared into his room.

Just as Little Lola had settled into her hammock and I had stolen a hot dog from the hot dog stand in her room there was a knock on the door. She jumped out of bed and answered it. It was Dr. Science and Asha. She let them in and the three of them began to talk.

"Something is funny about that guy," Dr. Science said.

"I think he's nice," Asha said.

"So do I," added Lola.

"You two don't understand. Why is he keeping us here? He knows something is going on with us. He might even know Little Lola has The Green Dragon."

"Do you really think so?" Asha asked.

"Why else would he want us to stay in his mansion? It's surely not for our company. We're complete strangers," Dr. Science said.

"Maybe he's just a lonely, old guy who wants some friends. You heard his story about being shunned," Asha said.

"That was just a bunch of silly **prose**, Asha. We've got to get out of here and quickly too. We've got to leave before he discovers that Lola has The Green Dragon and wants to take it away. Don't you understand that our safety is **pending**?"

"Finders keepers," Little Lola said with a little yawn.

Suddenly, the door swung wide open. Klaus Von Bonbon was standing there with Otto Pearlbutton and both were holding swords.

"So, you've found us out," Von Bonbon shouted.

"We have indeed and we're leaving," Dr. Science shouted back and grabbed the hammock Lola had been sleeping in.

"Come, come, Dr. Science, you really think that little hammock with protect you from our swords?" Otto Pearlbutton asked as he advanced toward Little Lola. Again, I'd found myself in a strange situation. In order to protect The Green Dragon I'd have to protect Little Lola. I ran toward Pearlbutton with my claws outstretched and with a flash I scratched his face leaving a nasty **laceration**. Pearlbutton dropped his sword and held the cut on his face. Asha Bloom quickly took the sword and began fighting off Klaus Von Bonbon while Dr. Science fashioned the hammock and some bed sheets into a kind of kite.

"Take that," Asha said as she shoved Klaus Von Bonbon out of the room with the heel of her fantastic red pumps and slammed the door shut.

"Quickly Asha, come over here," Dr. Science demanded. She ran over to him and took hold of the kite he'd made as I grabbed Little Lola and pulled her to the window. With a **heave** we managed to get the heavy window opened just as Klaus Von Bonbon burst once more into the room. We all jumped out of the window, holding onto the hammock for dear life as we sailed away.

Fill in the Blank

Choose the word that best completes each of the following sentences.

1. Jason's two left feet made him very _____ during intense games of dodge ball.

   a. fickle

   b. tarnished

   c. vulnerable

   d. nasty

2. Harriet had a/an _____ to her mother to baby sit her younger brother.

   a. obligation

   b. chore

   c. idea

   d. fit

3. Mark left the poetry reading early because he thought that the readers were _____.

   a. unintelligent

   b. insipid

   c. tired

   d. cliché

4. Many thought it was a _____ idea of Jimmy's to free the frogs from the science lab.

   a. radical

   b. brilliant

   c. naughty

   d. hilarious

5. Some say that a black cat is a very bad _____.

   a. pet

   b. swimmer

   c. temper

   d. omen

6. It is best to be as respectful as you can while walking through a cemetery, because many people consider it _____ ground.

   a. spooky

   b. deathly

   c. hallowed

   d. peaceful

7. Peggy won her debate with a brilliant _____.

   a. speech

   b. rebuttal

   c. imitation

   d. cheer

8. Jerry decided to give up his life in an office in exchange for wandering the globe as a/an _____.

   a. nomad

   b. explorer

   c. archeologist

   d. medicine man

9. _____ is a very painful disease that typically effect the joints in the hands and feet.

   a. Cancer

   b. Cooties

   c. Gout

   d. Chicken Pox

10. In order to _____ the problem she'd caused in the lunch room, Amy was made to apologize in front of the whole school.

    a. forget

    b. see

    c. define

    d. rectify

11. Owls are typically considered to be _____ creatures.

    a. flying

    b. nocturnal

    c. large

    d. fierce

12. Failing a test can have _____ consequences on your overall grades.

    a. sad

    b. unhelpful

    c. disgusting

    d. grave

13. History proves that the English Navy stood _____ against the Spanish Armada.

    a. terrified

    b. resolute

    c. stubborn

    d. hasty

14. Oddly, Bernie thought he was starting to _____ when hair started growing on his upper lip.

    a. die

    b. grow

    c. mutate

    d. crack up

15. Despite his previous tricks, it wasn't easy to spot Jack's cunning use of _____ to get his own way.

    a. guile

    b. intelligence

    c. language

    d. magic

16. Joseph loved and _____ his grandparents.

    a. teased

    b. revered

    c. hated

    d. fought with

17. Detectives are always looking for a _____ when someone has committed a crime.

    a. reason

    b. fingerprint

    c. weapon

    d. motive

18. Alice performed her dance routine with a lot of _____.

   a. mistakes

   b. gusto

   c. laughter

   d. costumes

19. Diana was upset when Jane _____ at her idea to have a bake sale.

   a. smiled

   b. lied

   c. scoffed

   d. jeered

20. To sneak into the film premier, Harry told the security guard that was a journalist and a member of the _____.

   a. crew

   b. media

   c. gang

   d. organization

Relationships

Decide what type of relationship the words below have to each other. If the words have similar meanings, write "S" next to the pair of words. If they have different or opposite meanings, write "O" next to the words.

1. repent :: sin
2. servile :: bossy
3. matriarch :: mother
4. exploit :: manipulate
5. shrewd :: idiotic
6. emerge :: appear
7. snide :: sweet
8. malice :: dislike
9. ecstasy :: pleasure
10. spat :: fight
11. malignant :: harmless
12. earmark :: tag
13. subdue :: control
14. lull :: annoy
15. decoy :: imitation
16. supernatural :: mysterious
17. perpendicular :: horizontal
18. decapitate :: behead
19. torment :: abuse
20. precarious :: secure

True or False

Decide whether the following statements are True or False about Chapter 1. If the statement is true, write a "T" next to it. If the statement is false, write an "F" next to it.

1. Frederick P. Honeycutt left a prosaic account of how he used The Green Dragon in his diary.
2. Dr. Science discovers the exact location of where they've landed when he finds a levee on the map he keeps in his lab coat.
3. Otto Pearlbutton falls out the window and becomes a paraplegic.
4. Klaus Von BonBon tries to impair his guests' judgment by spoiling them with whatever they desire.
5. In the evening the walls in the dining room turn from a shade of yellow to a pale color of white.
6. Klaus Von BonBon does not take a patronizing tone with any of his guests.
7. Dr. Science is very good at putting together makeshift ways of escaping.
8. The Green Dragon offers immunity to any who are in its presence.
9. When they follow Klaus Von BonBon to his mansion Dr. Science, Little Lola, Asha Bloom,

and The Cat are offered the best accommodations.

10. Pending a note from his mother, Klaus Von BonBon will legally inherit The Green Dragon.

11. Little Lola has an insatiable thirst for orange soda.

12. Asha Bloom does not find her room satisfactory.

13. Instead of going to bed the guests at Klaus Von BonBon's mansion all stay up and perform a pantomime for their host.

14. The Cat has innate spy instincts that usually lead him in the right direction.

15. Otto Pearlbutton is captivated by Asha Bloom's beauty.

16. In order to escape Dr. Science and The Cat have to heave a table in front of the front door.

17. The Cat finds that he is very capable of reading Frederick P. Honeycutt's diary by the embers of the fire in the sitting room.

18. Klaus Von BonBon is a very sweet and jovial host who cares for nothing but the comfort of his guests.

Relationships

Decide what type of relationship the words below have to each other. If the words have similar meanings, write "S" next to the pair of words. If they have different or opposite meanings, write "O" next to the words.

1. deplete :: consume
2. tycoon :: boss
3. dignity :: lowliness
4. ulcer :: sore
5. profuse :: sparse
6. cumbersome :: easy
7. unconscious :: awake
8. propaganda :: promotion
9. corpse :: living person
10. prose :: poetry
11. beholden :: obligated
12. prestige :: rank
13. maternal :: paternal
14. preoccupied :: busy
15. laceration :: wound
16. atrocious :: elegant
17. persecute :: protect
18. lament :: complain
19. pauper :: rich person
20. casualty :: accident

CHAPTER 6
Live or Let Joust

If you think floating from Belize to a mansion in the Pyrenees on a bubble is **turbulent**, you should try flying through the air with only a hammock and a bed sheet keeping you from falling to a **premature** death. Instead of landing on the ground safely, Dr. Science, Asha Bloom, Little Lola, and myself got tangled up in the hammock when it caught on a tree branch. Needless to say, when you make a flying machine out of a hammock and bed sheet and it gets caught in a tree, it can become something of a net. In fact, in its tangling it had become a very convincing net. Being stuck in this net in a tree, instead of being free on the ground, caused a bit of **discord** among Dr. Science, Asha, and Lola. While I tried to remain **dispassionate** and think of away out of the mess the three of them started arguing.

"Way to go, Dr. Science, your hammock idea officially messed up my hair and got us stuck in a dumb, old tree," Asha started.

"Asha, this is really no time to be thinking about your hair," Dr. Science replied, **alluding** to her constant **superficiality**.

"Yeah, you're right, maybe I should be thinking about your **blatant** stupidity. I should start calling you Dr. Stupid instead of Dr. Science."

"As if you're some kind of genius, Asha," Little Lola said joining into the argument.

"Shut up, you **inept**, little freak," Asha screamed back.

"You think you're so great, Asha. You think you're always so pretty and fashionable and smart, but really you're just a—" Before Lola could finish her **barrage** of insults at Asha Bloom I'd managed to cut a hole in the bottom of the hammock with one of my claws and we all fell to the ground. Dr. Science quickly hopped to his feet and brushed the leaves from his white lab coat, Asha fixed her hair, and Little Lola checked underneath her cap to see that The Green Dragon was still safe before she picked me up and snuggled me to her chest.

Dr. Science cleared his throat and tried to **muster** an apology, but Asha and Lola gave him a look that told him it wasn't necessary. It was quiet for a few minutes before anyone said anything. Finally, Asha said, "So, where do you think we are?"

Dr. Science had taken out his maps and was looking around at all the trees. "It appears as if we've landed in a **dense** forest of some sort, which if you look closely at my map is located right here."

"Oh goody! We've landed in France," Asha said, looking at where Dr. Science was pointing. "When can we go shopping? I love shopping in France."

"I don't want to **agitate** you, Asha, but I don't think you'll be able to do much shopping any time soon," Dr. Science said, pointing at the trees.

"Good, I hate shopping," Lola said. "When can we go on a roller coaster? I love roller coasters. Do they have roller coasters in France?"

"Let me be **candid** with you both," Dr. Science finally said looking up from his map. "We're lost in a rather large forest and, until we find our way to some kind of town, there won't be any shopping or any roller coasters. Not to mention, we still need to figure out how to make The Green Dragon work."

"Perhaps we should try it now," Asha said snatching the cap off Little Lola's head. The Green Dragon fell to Lola's feet and green sparks started flying everywhere.

"Asha, stop that! The Green Dragon is not a toy," Dr. Science yelled while Little Lola quickly picked it up and held it tightly in her hands to stop the sparks from flying.

"Yeah, stop it, Asha. And give me back my cap," Lola demanded.

As Asha gave Little Lola back her cap the three of them stood in a circle and looked at The Green Dragon while I wandered around them trying to get a better view. I sneaked into the middle of their tight circle and looked up into Little Lola's hands which were outstretched so that everyone could get a good look at what was happening. A green tornado began to spin inside the emerald, twirling faster and faster, keeping us all transfixed. Then, right behind us we heard a twig snap. Little Lola slipped The Green Dragon back under her cap just as a loud voice shouted, "Who goes there?"

None of us really knew what to answer and finally when the voice demanded that we identify ourselves for the third time Dr. Science answered. "We mean no harm. We are lost in this forest and looking for the closest town."

"The closest town isn't for miles," a sweeter voice said, and suddenly we could see from whom the voices were coming. An **obese** man with a crown on his head and a woman wearing the wrong shade of lipstick appeared from out of nowhere.

"I'm King Bruce and this is my girlfriend Veronica," the man with the crown on his head said.

"King…king of what?" Asha asked **belligerently**.

"King of this forest," King Bruce said back with a **benevolent** look on his face.

"Who made you King?" Little Lola asked curiously.

"I did," replied Veronica. "And you have to do whatever we say."

"Yes, whatever we say because this is our forest and you're in it without an invitation," King Bruce said. Veronica gave him a little poke as if to remind him of something. "Oh yeah," the supposed king added while he cleared his throat, "it **behooves** me to tell you that you're all under arrest."

"For what?" Dr. Science asked.

Veronica looked him up and down and took out a long, sharp sword. "For treason, of course."

"Treason? How could we have committed treason? That's impossible," Dr. Science said defensively.

"OK, if you don't like treason," Veronica said, "it can be for something else, I guess. How about trying to put an **embargo** on peanut butter shipped to the forest?"

"Good one, Veronica," King Bruce said and gave her a high five.

"Thank you, your majesty," Veronica said, blushing a little bit.

"This is absolutely ridiculous. How can you **abstractly** just come up with a reason to arrest us?" Dr. Science asked.

"Because it's our forest," King Bruce answered. "Now come on, off to prison with the lot of you."

Perhaps it was the fact that if we followed the two **lunatics** we might have a better idea of finding out where we were, or maybe it was the fact that both of them were carrying rather sharp swords, but either way, and with slight **resignation**, the four of us stood up and went with King Bruce and his girlfriend Veronica to their so-called prison in their so-called kingdom.

The prison looked more like a **dormitory** than a prison. It had the feel of a summer camp cabin with rows of cots and insects flying overhead. The windows were all open and there was a nice breeze blowing. If you listened closely you could even hear a nearby stream babbling. The four of us were forced inside and while we all looked around at our new surroundings I noticed that there were other prisoners in this so-called prison as well. One of them came out from under a cot and looked nervously at us. Then others started to show themselves when they realized that we were prisoners instead of **associates** of King Bruce. Finally, the first one who crawled out from under his cot came over and introduced himself. "Hello there, I'm Goldenblake Williams," he said, **extending** a hand to Dr. Science.

"I'm Dr. Science, and this is Asha Bloom, Little Lola, and her pet cat," Dr. Science said, shaking Goldenblake William's hand.

"What did they get you for?" a woman said as she came over towards us.

"What do you mean 'get us for?'" Asha asked.

"I mean why did King Bruce **incarcerate** you?" the woman said trying to **clarify** her question.

"Treason," Little Lola said.

"Actually, it was an embargo on peanut butter," Dr. Science corrected.

"Oh yeah, it was peanut butter, wasn't it?" Lola responded, nodding her head.

"What are all of you doing in here?" Asha asked while sitting down on a cot near an open window.

Goldenblake Williams answered first, "I'm here because I'm a suspected **cannibal**, but really I don't even eat meat—I'm a **vegetarian**."

"And I'm here because of some **amorous conspiracy**. I supposedly tried to take King Bruce's affection away from Veronica," the woman said, started laughing a little bit. "As if I'd ever consider doing something like that with King Bruce, that's just disgusting. By the way, my name is Maude Peeblesworth."

"And I'm Hamilton Jambon," a voice said from behind a curtain that had been put up so that everyone could have a bit of privacy when they dressed. The man emerged wearing a light blue and white striped suit and a pressed white, cotton shirt. Everything about him was clean and **tailored** except his hair which sat messily atop his head like Dr. Science's. "I'm accused of being a **glutton** because I stole all of King Bruce's cheese one afternoon at a tea party. Can you believe that? So utterly unfair."

Hamilton had been in the so-called prison the longest of any of the others. He **estimated** that he'd been there for at least three years, but it was hard to tell due to the lack of clocks and calendars. Ms. Peeblesworth had arrived in the prison sometime after Hamilton and Williams had been the last to arrive until the four of us joined them. It was obvious that they were happy for the new company. It seemed that life was rather tedious under the **domain** of King Bruce and Veronica.

After a long discussion of how **bleak** life was in prison, Asha stood up and looked out the window. She could see King Bruce and Veronica pretending as if they were on some sort of **expedition**. Each of them were using long, thick sticks and pretending that they were ponies as the galloped around **brandishing** their swords and looking under rocks. As Asha looked on with a **grimace** hidden behind her big sunglasses, King Bruce's playtime was interrupted by the sound of screeching brakes and the appearance of a large delivery truck. "Sounds like the delivery is here," Goldenblake said, getting up from his cot where he was staring at the wooden ceiling beams.

"The delivery truck?" Dr. Science asked.

"Once a week we get a delivery from the local market," Hamilton answered.

"King Bruce and Veronica like to **degrade** us by making us unload the truck, but what they don't realize is we take all the good stuff and hide it in here while they're not looking," Maude added with a smile. "I've got a collection of peanut butter because it's my favorite. Goldenblake likes to **hoard** all the baked goods. And as for Hamilton, he's known for stealing cheese."

While Little Lola laughed at the notion that the three prisoners were playing a fantastic prank on King Bruce and Veronica, loud steps approached the so-called prison doors. They swung open and there in all his fake glory stood King Bruce. "All right, you lot get out here and unpack the truck while I take tea with Veronica and the **ambassador**."

"Who's the ambassador?" Asha whispered to Maude.

"He's the delivery man from the market. King Bruce and Veronica pretend he's an ambassador from another town bringing them gifts and news from different places. They treat him like some kind of **herald**, but he's really just a truck driver and I think he makes up most of the news he tells them," Maude answered quietly.

Asha tried not to laugh as she and the rest of the prisoners filed out of the so-called prison one by one and headed toward the delivery truck. A tall man got out of the drivers seat and greeted King Bruce and Veronica with a high-five and the three of them disappeared to enjoy the **rite** of afternoon tea. Dr. Science looked around while Hamilton and Goldenblake started to unload the back of the truck. "Call me **delirious** or crazy or whatever you want, but why aren't we escaping right now? No one is watching. It would be rather easy. If a delivery truck can make it here I'm sure we're in near **proximity** to a town. We can just follow the path from the tire tracks," Dr. Science stated.

"Dr. Science, escaping would be incredibly **hazardous**," Maude said.

"How could it be that bad?" Asha asked, adding her voice to the **dissent**.

Before he answered Goldenblake, Williams looked around to see if anyone was in **earshot** of them. "It isn't the prison that is our prison—it's the forest," he said.

"What are you talking about? The forest can't be that big and scary. It's just a bunch of trees," Asha said in response.

"Trust him, Asha. The forest is no place to go wandering," Maude added while trying to **hamper** her voice so that King Bruce and his tea party couldn't hear her.

Before Asha, or anyone for that matter, could say anything else they were interrupted by Veronica. "What are you talking about over there?" she shouted **callously**. "There will be absolutely less talking and more **rigorous** unloading of the truck!"

"Yes, indeed," **derided** King Bruce in a shout louder than Veronica's. We continued our **strenuous manual** labor until the truck had been unloaded and all the tea had been finished. King Bruce then pretended to get on his horse that was really a stick and galloped over toward us. He took his sword and pointed it in the direction of the so-called prison and demanded that we march back in single file.

Once the door was closed and then locked by King Bruce, we heard the loud truck's engine start up again and as it drove off we all started to relax a bit more. "What little **memento** did you manage to bring with you, Hamilton?" asked Maude.

"Ms. Peeblesworth, I don't appreciate you **insinuating** that I'm a thief, but if you must know I've taken a large and **scrumptious** cut of good English cheddar. And you?"

Maude held up a jar of peanut butter with a big smile on her face before she asked Goldenblake what he took. "What about you Mr. Williams? Have you got anything **noteworthy** or **lucrative**?"

"I'm afraid what I took isn't worth a penny, Maude."

The smile on Maude's face began to **falter** before she dared to ask what it was that Goldenblake had gotten his hands on.

"Let me **allay** your fears. I've taken the ambassador's map," Goldenblake Williams said triumphantly. Dr. Science, Asha Bloom, Little Lola, and I all rushed over toward him to view the small piece of paper that was in his hands. "Now we can escape."

"But Goldenblake," Maude said a little scared, "we can't possibly escape. What about the forest."

"Maude, Dr. Science, and Asha are right. We've got to stop being so scared and **complacent**," Goldenblake said.

"Here, here," Hamilton agreed with his mouth full of cheddar. "I'm all for escape as soon as I finish this fine cheese."

Sadly, Maude didn't agree with either of them. "I cannot **endorse** this. Escape into the forest and your deaths will **ensue**."

"Don't be such a ninny, Maude," Hamilton Jambon said, offering her a nice slice of his cheese. "If you come with us I'll show you where to get the best cheeses in all of France."

"Although cheese is a very tasty **incentive**, Hamilton, I just don't think it's very wise idea. You know what's out there. You know that if we even dare leave this cabin that King Bruce will use The Green Dragon to kill us."

"Aren't you tired of being **censored** all the time, Maude? Aren't you bored with being told when you can and can't talk, when you can and can't eat, when you can and can't laugh? Who knows if The Green Dragon even exists? King Bruce is crazy and Veronica isn't far off from that. They gallop around pretending to be riding horses when they're sticks for goodness sake," Goldenblake said, trying to boost her emotional **stamina**.

"Give me cheese or give me death," Hamilton said, standing on one of the cots like a general trying to **rally** his troops.

Dr. Science finally **interjected**, "I for one am not afraid of any silly little dragon and I do not want to stay in this **forsaken** cabin any longer than I have to."

"I agree with Dr. Science," Asha said.

"Me too," Little Lola said, knowing that if she stayed in the cabin there'd be a serious lack of orange soda.

"Good," Goldenblake continued, "then what we need is a leader and a plan."

"I **nominate** Dr. Science," Asha said, quickly elbowing Little Lola.

"Ouch," Little Lola shouted before understanding why Asha had elbowed her. "I second the nomination and so does my little kitten."

Hamilton Jambon and Goldenblake Williams both agreed that Dr. Science should be the leader of the **evacuation** plans and, as we sat around **brainstorming** ideas of how best to **distract** King Bruce and his ugly girlfriend Veronica, Maude Peeblesworth finally agreed to join us in our escape.

OOOOOOOOOOOO

Once Maude Peeblesworth had decided to join us she became a planning **fanatic**.

She made sure we all understood the most **acute** details of the camp we'd been imprisoned in and each and every **facet** of King Bruce and Veronica's relationship. Apparently, she'd been observing them for ages noticing each and every fight they'd had since she'd been taken prisoner. Typically, their fights were caused by the **orthodox** things that other couples fought about: one not paying enough attention to the other, money problems, stealing the covers at night, etc. But when it came to restoring **equilibrium** to their relationship, instead of the customary **doting** that most couples practice, they would **joust**. King Bruce would get on his pretend horse and Veronica would get on hers. Then they would run at each other at top speed until one of them was lying in an **incoherent** heap on the ground. Once the joust's loser came back to their senses they were made to apologize and **normalcy** was restored, if you can call that normal.

"This is all very interesting," Dr. Science said, "but how is it going to help us escape?"

"Don't you see," Hamilton Jambon said finishing his cheddar, "if we can cause a **rift** between King Bruce and the hideous Veronica, then they'll be so distracted jousting that we can escape without them even noticing."

"Yes, but how can we get them to be upset with each other? I mean, look at them," Asha said pointing to the two of them out the window. King Bruce and Veronica had snuggled up together on a bench swing and were pinching each others' noses "They're in their own little love **niche**."

"What does King Bruce love more than anything in the world?" Goldenblake asked with a gleam in his eye.

Maude smiled and began to nod up and down. "Peanut butter," she answered.

"And who among us is a well-known and **laudable** peanut butter thief?" Goldenblake continued.

"Maude Peeblesworth," replied Hamilton Jambon loudly.

"Precisely," Goldenblake said, beaming at everyone.

"I see where you're going with this, Mr. Williams," Dr Science said, "but we're in **limbo** here and we've got to have a better plan than just peanut butter."

Everyone agreed that just having a stash of King Bruce's favorite **substance** really wasn't enough to escape. It wasn't like we could trade the peanut butter for our freedom or dangle it in front of his face with a string. Somehow we needed to come up with an **innovative** plan. They sat around discussing different strategies, some with a lot of **merit** and some with a lot of **defects**.

"We could **indict** King Bruce for our false imprisonment and then cover him in peanut butter so he's too sticky to chase us," Maude suggested.

"I think one of us should disguise ourselves in that **opaque**, purple cape Veronica is always wearing and hide the peanut butter under her bed so that it looks like she stole it," Hamilton said.

"Neither of those plans are bad, perhaps if we **condense** the two we'll come up with something a little less **ambiguous**," said Dr. Science.

"Whatever you **deem** best, doctor. You're the boss," Goldenblake said and gave him a rather **benign** pat on the back.

Eventually we came up with a very involved plan. As soon as King Bruce and Veronica had fallen asleep,

Little Lola and I would sneak into their cabin. Once we were there we would spread the peanut butter all around Veronica's mouth and fingers and leave and leave a few empty jars of it around her side of the bed. It would make her look like to one who had been stealing all of the peanut butter! Then we'd hide the leftover jars of peanut butter underneath her purple cape with a few of the labels showing just enough to cause **suspicion**. Of course, we didn't know if our trick would work or if we would have to take some **ulterior** course of action later on, but we were all certainly willing to give it a try. Our first step seemed easy enough, though: We had to eat a few of the jars of peanut butter.

I think peanut butter is delicious, but all good things have a limit. After each of us had eaten so much peanut butter that the tops of our mouths were sticking to the bottoms, we finally saw the lights go off in King Bruce and Veronica's cabin. It wouldn't be long until it was time for Little Lola and I to sneak over and complete step two of our plan. We waited for an hour to make sure that King Bruce and Veronica were completely asleep, and then loaded our arms full of the stolen peanut butter. There was no room for mistakes. If we were caught all of us would suffer **morbid** consequences.

I have to admit that although she's a criminal, Little Lola would make a rather good spy. The two of us sneaked over to King Bruce and Veronica's cabin without making a noise. Little Lola was in charge of finding the purple cape and I was to smear the peanut butter all over Veronica. The weather that night was **sultry** which made the peanut butter extra gooey and easy to spread. Thankfully, both King Bruce and Veronica slept like logs, so it wasn't difficult to finish our plan. As we hurried back to the so-called prison Lola hugged me tightly while licking peanut butter off her fingers. We quickly entered the cabin and shut the door behind us. Maude Peeblesworth, Goldenblake Williams, Hamilton Jambon, and Asha Bloom were waiting for us by a window and when we quickly entered the cabin and shut the door behind us they let out an **unbridled** cheer. Even Dr. Science seemed excited to see that we'd returned successfully. But we couldn't celebrate for too long as the noise from the cheer had woken up King Bruce who could probably be heard for miles.

○○○○○○○○○○○○

"VERONICA," King Bruce yelled. "VERONICA, YOU ARE COVERED IN PEANUT BUTTER!"

"What are you talking about?" Veronica asked sleepily.

"YOU HAVE EATEN ALL OF MY PEANUT BUTTER! YOU ARE THE THIEF!"

"I'm the what?" Veronica asked again, this time sitting up and opening her eyes to try and **verify** what King Bruce was shouting about. She was indeed covered in peanut butter. It was on her fingers, around her mouth, there was even a little bit in her hair. It was very confusing to her and she found herself completely **disoriented**. She'd gone to bed right after her bath and now she'd woken up covered in sticky peanut butter.

How could this have happened? She thought that she must be dreaming.

As she pinched herself to try to wake up from this horrible and messy nightmare, King Bruce saw something underneath her purple cape and stomped toward it. He yanked the cape from its place and revealed the other jars of peanut butter. "HOW COULD YOU?" he screamed. "ALL OF MY BELOVED PEANUT BUTTER!" He sat down and started to cry like a little kid. While he sobbed Veronica got out of bed and went over to him.

"Bruce, you must believe that this wasn't me. I didn't take your peanut butter."

"YOU LIAR! AND THAT'S KING BRUCE TO YOU! JUST LOOK AT ALL THIS PEANUT BUTTER! IT MUST BE AT LEAST A YEAR'S WORTH! I SHOULD LOCK YOU UP IN THE PRISON!"

Veronica did not take kindly to that suggestion at all and her face changed from its typical red color to some incredibly unnatural **pallor**. It was one thing to be accused of stealing peanut butter, but it was another to be told she should be locked up in a so-called prison with a bunch of commoners. She refused to think that her **legacy** would be the woman who had the heart of King Bruce until she was locked up in a so-called prison for supposedly stealing peanut butter. It was absolutely out of the question. "I challenge you to a joust, King Bruce."

"A JOUST," King Bruce shouted. "WE'LL HAVE A JOUST AT DAWN!"

Back in the so-called prison we were all very delighted that our plan had worked, but we also knew that we had quite a bit of work to do before the joust at dawn. This time there would be no bubble gum or hammock kites to help us escape—we'd have to go it on our own and on foot. Dr. Science gathered his maps and put them in the special hidden pocket inside his white lab coat. Asha Bloom polished her sunglasses. Maude Peeblesworth tried to figure out how to put one last jar of peanut butter in her purse. Hamilton Jambon shoved piece after piece of cheese in his pockets. Goldenblake Williams took a little nap. And Little Lola checked to see that The Green Dragon was still safe under her cap. It made her very curious as to why everyone was so frightened of it. She'd been wearing it under her cap for days and although she thought it was pretty she didn't think it was much to **marvel** over. She did, however, understand that it was a powerful bargaining chip and that as long as she had it under her cap she'd be able to get what she wanted. Maybe she'd trade it for a lifetime supply of orange soda. Maybe she'd trade it to Asha for a pair of fancy sunglasses or to Dr. Science for one of his forged pieces of priceless art. As she stroked me and thought about these things the sun started to come up and we all knew that we'd soon be making a run for it from the so-called prison.

When we heard the door to King Bruce and Veronica's cabin swing open, we knew that the time had come. We waited for both of them to march out to the open field near their cabin. King Bruce appeared first and then **beckoned** Veronica to follow. "You have

squandered all of my precious peanut butter and now you will pay," he said to her as she stood lifted her leg over a stick she was using as a pretend pony.

"I did nothing of the sort," she replied.

While King Bruce and Veronica stared each other down across the field, the seven of us quietly sneaked out one of the windows of the so-called prison and ran to hide behind a large tree. "OK," Dr. Science said pointing to the map that Goldenblake Williams had stolen from the truck driver, "we made it here to this large tree and we need to run in that direction. That is the direction of the town." We all nodded silently and one by one took off running. Maude Peeblesworth went first, then Hamilton Jambon, and then Goldenblake Williams. As they ran to safety there was suddenly a loud thud. The jar of peanut butter from Maude's purse fell onto the ground. It was loud enough to distract King Bruce and Veronica from their joust and they ran over to inspect what was happening.

"OUR PRISONERS! THEY'VE ESCAPED," King Bruce shouted.

"WELL, DON'T JUST STAND THERE," Veronica joined in, "GET THEM!"

Asha, Lola, Dr. Science, and I had no other choice but to run the opposite way of the others. King Bruce was after us swinging around his sharp sword and yelling. Just as he was about to grab me by the tail a boomerang shaped slice of cheese came whizzing through the air and hit him in the head. We knew, of course, that Hamilton Jambon had used his last scraps of cheese to make the boomerang and thrown it at King Bruce in a **scrupulous** attempt at helping us escape. Sadly, we could only hope that the three other prisoners had made it to safety, because we never heard or saw them again. They'd run one way and we'd been forced to run the other. With King Bruce knocked out cold on the forest floor and Veronica completely out of sight, the four of us ran as fast as we could away from our captors.

Relationships

Decide what type of relationship the words below have to each other. If the words have similar meanings, write "S" next to the pair of words. If they have different or opposite meanings, write "O" next to the words.

19. obese :: overweight
20. clarify :: confuse
21. acute :: unimportant
22. domain :: kingdom
23. marvel :: disregard
24. abstract :: conceptual
25. vegetarian :: carnivore
26. dormitory :: bedroom
27. memento :: souvenir
28. elude :: confront
29. barrage :: bombardment
30. embargo :: allowance
31. merit :: fault
32. dote :: ignore
33. tailored :: custom-made
34. insinuate :: hint
35. morbid :: cheerful
36. niche :: nook
37. scrumptious :: disgusting
38. beckon :: repel

Matching

Match each word on the left to a word with the similar meaning on the right.

1. endorse a. impudent
2. nominate b. guess
3. behoove c. early
4. ensue d. harmless
5. opaque e. designate
6. belligerent f. aspect
7. equilibrium g. kind
8. orthodox h. impenetrable
9. benevolent i. nearness
10. estimate j. stumble
11. pallor k. authorize
12. benign l. depressing
13. expedition m. start
14. premature n. necessary
15. blatant o. paleness
16. facet p. journey
17. proximity q. ordinary
18. bleak r. tradition
19. falter s. obvious
20. rite t. balance

Fill in the Blank

Choose the word that best completes each of the following sentences.

1. Kenneth tried very hard to _____ the courage to take his math test.

   a. finish

   b. discover

   c. muster

   d. fake

2. Fiona tried to _____ her friend's fear of snakes.

   a. allay

   b. aggravate

   c. justify

   d. tease

3. It is not nice to _____ anyone for looking different.

   a. cheer

   b. deride

   c. punch

   d. scorn

4. It is _____ to donate money to charity.

   a. fickle

   b. cheap

   c. heartfelt

   d. laudable

5. Karl's _____ were not well thought of among the rest of the school.

   a. people

   b. associates

   c. pets

   d. gang

6. It is best not to _____ your parents if you want something from them.

   a. find

   b. ask

   c. trick

   d. agitate

7. Mary was unhappy due to the amount of _____ she had caused with her friends.

   a. jousting

   b. playing

   c. discord

   d. fault

8. The _____ the football team left behind was a very good one.

   a. flag

   b. legacy

   c. uniform

   d. reputation

9. When the bell rings to let school out many students act like complete _____.

    a. lunatics

    b. geniuses

    c. monkeys

    d. savages

10. Daphne was very happy to be chosen as her school's _____ to visit New York City.

    a. cheerleader

    b. debate team captain

    c. flute player

    d. ambassador

11. Mr. Hayward's chemistry quizzes had a tendency to _____ his students.

    a. enrage

    b. fail

    c. disorient

    d. shame

12. Being in a fight with two of your best friends will most likely put you in a position of
_____.

   a. limbo

   b. sadness

   c. boredom

   d. anger

13. _____ a warm welcome to new students is always a nice thing to do.

   a. Showing

   b. Faking

   c. Making

   d. Extending

14. When writing a research report it is best to be specific about the topic rather than _____.

   a. boring

   b. ambiguous

   c. uneducated

   d. realistic

15. There's nothing worse than a _____ politician.

    a. dispassionate

    b. nerdy

    c. competent

    d. rotten

16. Sam thought it would be _____ to put half of his allowance into a savings account.

    a. good

    b. brilliant

    c. lucrative

    d. stupid

17. If you get caught robbing a bank you will most likely be _____.

    a. rewarded

    b. slapped

    c. laughed at

    d. incarcerated

18. Mrs. Smith was feeling very _____ because it was Valentine's Day.

    a. chilly

    b. amorous

    c. hyper

    d. happy

19. In America, the 1960s were full of voices of revolutionary _____.

    a. cries

    b. shouting

    c. dissent

    d. feeling

20. Pulling weeds can be very rough _____ labor.

    a. tiring

    b. manual

    c. boring

    d. hot

Matching

Match each word on the left to a word with the similar meaning on the right.

1. callous	a. honest
2. fanatic	b. man-eater
3. rigorous	c. dangerous
4. candid	d. difficult
5. glutton	e. press together
6. resignation	f. save
7. cannibal	g. messenger
8. grimace	h. overenthusiastic
9. scrupulous	i. limit
10. censor	j. vitality
11. hamper	k. burdensome
12. stamina	l. plot
13. complacent	m. waste
14. hazardous	n. overeater
15. squander	o. heartless
16. condense	p. giving up
17. herald	q. frown
18. strenuous	r. impede
19. conspiracy	s. contented
20. hoard	t. principled

Relationships

Decide what type of relationship the words below have to each other. If the words have similar meanings, write "S" next to the pair of words. If they have different or opposite meanings, write "O" next to the words.

1. sultry :: hot
2. deem :: consider
3. incentive :: deterrent
4. superficial :: fake
5. defect :: perfection
6. incoherent :: aware
7. turbulent :: smooth
8. degrade :: shame
9. indict :: charge
10. ulterior :: known
11. delirious :: conscious
12. inept :: incapable
13. unbridled :: moderate
14. dense :: thick
15. innovative :: unoriginal
16. verify :: disprove
17. noteworthy :: insignificant
18. rally :: disband
19. interject :: intrude
20. forsaken :: cast off

21. brainstorm :: think
22. evacuate :: stay put
23. distract :: focus
24. joust :: duel
25. normalcy :: unordinary
26. rift :: fight
27. substance :: object

CHAPTER 7

Forgery From the Black Lagoon

Tunnels are funny things, especially if you find yourself falling through one which is what happened to Dr. Science, Asha Bloom, Little Lola, and me as we were running away from King Bruce and his not so **lenient** girlfriend Veronica. The four of us were running so quickly that none of us really noticed the rather big hole in the ground. Asha tumbled first, then Dr. Science, and then Little Lola and I. As we fell toward the bottom I could hear King Bruce and Veronica arguing above us and I felt a little lucky to be tumbling in the darkness rather than being **lynched** and taken to the **gallows** by the two of them. They were both so crazy that there really was no telling what would have happened if they'd actually captured us again. I, for one, was happy not to have to find out.

We reached the bottom of the tunnel with four large splashes. We couldn't see a thing, but we knew we were lucky the water had broken our fall. It was **pitch** black and the water was very cold. Of course, being the **pragmatic** one of the group, Dr. Science searched around in the pocket inside his white lab coat and found a little green glow stick. He snapped its middle it began to omit a ghostly green glow. As our eyes adjusted to the faint light, we found that we were in a lagoon surrounded by several large doors. One of the doors looked as if it was made of metal and had many dents in a circular pattern all around it. Another was painted with all sorts of colorful splotches as if someone had delicately thrown paint at it. Another door, Asha's favorite, was covered in jewels. She sat in front of it and smiled. And the last door was rather dull compared to the other three; it was wooden and had some sort of map carved into it.

Almost immediately Asha Bloom, Dr. Science, and Little Lola began to argue about which door to open. "Well, clearly we should open the one with the map because it will help us discover our way out of here," Dr. Science said.

"No," argued Little Lola, "we should open this one with all the splotches because it's the most interesting."

"Are both of you completely crazy? We should open the one with all these amazing jewels because it probably has even more jewels behind it," Asha said, touching the diamond-encrusted door knob.

Of course, when you're in any kind of crisis it's best to remain calm and see how the given situation presents itself. As the three of my companions continued to **hysterically** argue about which door to open, I decided it best to see which door would actually open. My first pick, the metal door, swung open.

"You see," Dr. Science said **pompously** to the others, "your doors are completely **irrelevant** now."

"Your door is now irrelevant, too," Lola pointed out while Asha was trying madly to **pry** open her jeweled door.

"Why won't it open?" she said, kicking it. "I want more jewels."

"Calm down," Dr. Science said. "Have you forgotten that we've found the ultimate jewel? We have The Green Dragon."

"You mean I have The Green Dragon," Little Lola said resentfully. It was obvious that she was sick of being considered as someone who just tagged along. "And if the two of you want to have anything to do with my emerald, then you're going to have to start showing me a little bit more respect." As she said this, Little Lola dusted the dirt from her sneakers, scooped me up into her arms, stood up very straight and tall, and marched right through the open doorway. Asha Bloom stood quietly with her mouth open as Dr. Science straightened the collar of his white lab coat. They looked at each other a little stunned and followed Lola through the door. After all, if they wanted The Green Dragon, there was nothing else they could do but follow her.

OOOOOOOOOOOO

Little Lola carried me for awhile but before the others caught up with us she put me down. It surprised me that the floor **underfoot** felt more like smooth marble than the rocks and dirt I was expecting. As we walked along in the dark we could hear Dr. Science and Asha Bloom walking quickly toward us. Little Lola had no **inclination** to stop and wait for them. She was sick of how they treated her. "Ya know what, kitty, I'm so sick and tired of those two always treating me like I'm some kind of **pathological** idiot. If anyone has got a case of the stupids, it's Asha. All she does is fix her hair and look at herself in the mirror. And as for Dr. Science, he was supposed to have stolen The Green Dragon before all this mess happened so that Asha and I could—"

before she could finish her **rant** we heard a noise and saw a light in front of us. Dr. Science and Asha must have seen the same thing because before too long they'd caught up to us.

Knowing that he'd never get The Green Dragon from Lola without apologizing, Dr. Science tried to smooth things over with her. "Lola, you shouldn't run off like that. You could get hurt and we wouldn't want you to get hurt. You're so important to us."

Sensing that Dr. Science's apology was completely **synthetic**, Lola said, "You two think I'm just some dumb kid. Well, this dumb kid isn't going to give you what you want. You can't have The Green Dragon."

Asha quickly thought it might be a good idea for her to try a different **tactic**. "Come on, Lola, don't be like that. You know we were worried. Why else do you think we came rushing after you? And besides, if either of us had wanted to we could have taken The Green Dragon from you already. What's most important is that the three of us stick together so that we can get it to the museum. You know that's been the plan this whole time." It seems that Asha's attempt to **placate** Little Lola worked much better than Dr. Science's. After Asha had finished her **plea** the three of them stood in the strange underground tunnel looking at the light in front of them and leaving their fight behind.

On one hand I was relieved that the three of them were getting along again because I could keep track of them a little easier, but on the other hand I was worried because three criminal minds working together are worse than one or two. I was also slightly taken aback by what Asha mentioned about getting The Green Dragon to a museum. Why on earth would she want to take one of the most valuable objects in the world to a museum? It didn't make any sense to me. The only thing I could imagine these three doing in a museum is **vandalizing** walls or stealing artwork—and they wouldn't need a priceless emerald for that. Another piece of their strange puzzle had fallen into my lap, and as we all walked toward the light in the tunnel, my mind began to race with difference **scenarios**. I was more than a little tired of their company. But **realistically**, the only way I'd ever find out what they were up to was to stick with them.

It was clear that as we walked toward the light in the tunnel that someone else was near. The closer we got the more voices we heard. Asha Bloom, Little Lola, and I approached the voices cautiously, but Dr. Science acted as if by being **reluctant** we were **procrastinating**. "Would you hurry up?" he said impatiently when we were mere feet from where the light was coming. He was acting quite strange, even for Dr. Science. It was as if he was **anticipating** something once we reached the light and all those voices. He was acting like he knew what was going to happen and by leading the way for the rest of us, it was obvious that he knew where he was.

When we'd finally reached the spot we heard a voice yell out, "Who's there?" The sound of the voice was actually kind of pleasant. It had a kind of **euphony** to it as if the person behind it had taken years and years of singing lessons. But when none of us answered the question the voice changed from pleasant to **obtrusive** and threatening. "If you value your lives, you'd best reveal who you are. Many lives had ended at that very spot on which you're standing. I demand that you tell me who you are or you will all be **inflicted** with terrible physical and **psychological trauma**."

"Sebastian, is that you?" asked Dr. Science while Asha Bloom and Little Lola looked at each other in complete shock. How did Dr. Science know who the voice was?

"Dr. Science?"

"Yes, it's me, Sebastian. Now stop this nonsense and let us in."

Suddenly, a large rock wall opened and bright light flooded the tunnel. A large room was revealed behind the wall and a young gentleman wearing jeans, a t-shirt, and sneakers came toward us. "Come on in and take a look around. Come see what we've done to the place since you left," the gentleman said.

"It looks as if you've been busy with those improvements I suggested, Sebastian," Dr. Science said.

"Um, excuse me," Asha finally said, "but before you two get all friendly and start to **reminisce**, would you mind telling me exactly what's going on?"

"Oh dear, how rude of me," said the gentleman. "I'm not very used to having guests."

"Sure, sure, but who are you? Where are we? Why do you live at the end of a tunnel?" Asha said as she started **interrogating** the young gentleman.

"My name is Sebastian Fresh and this is my hide-out."

"What are you hiding?" Little Lola asked while she looked around the large cave-like room. Her question amused both Dr. Science and Sebastian Fresh and they started to chuckle. The two of them obviously had a good **rapport** with each other.

"Look around you. What do you see?" Sebastian asked.

"I see a bunch of paintings and sculptures," Lola answered.

"And jewels," Asha added.

"Well then, there's your answer. We hide priceless works of art," Sebastian said and looked at Dr. Science before the two of them started to laugh again.

"I don't get it. What's so great about a bunch of paintings?" Lola asked **skeptically**. Her question caused Asha to join Dr. Science and Sebastian's laughter leaving Lola feeling **dejected**. While the three of them laughed at her, Lola's anger grew and grew. She didn't like feeling **ostracized**. It wasn't her fault she didn't know anything about art.

Sensing that Lola's temper was quickly reaching its **capacity**, Sebastian Fresh stopped laughing and offered to show her around. "Let me give you a grand tour, my new friend. I'll explain the whole operation."

Little Lola **vacillated** for a moment. Part of her just wanted to take The Green Dragon and leave Dr. Science and Asha Bloom behind in the tunnel, but the other part of her really wanted to understand why they'd come so far to end up in a tunnel full of art. Lola found herself in a **quandary**, but eventually made the decision to stick around because something inside told her that The Green Dragon would be more valuable if she could use it as a bargaining tool. Besides, if she left now Dr. Science and Asha Bloom would eventually hunt her down and steal the emerald from her anyway. Little Lola concluded that it was best to **reconcile** with the fact that Dr. Science and Asha Bloom were going to tease her, but it didn't really matter what any of them said because she had what they wanted in her hat. She took **refuge** in this knowledge, which allowed her terrible mood to **convalesce** and improve a great deal.

"I'm terribly sorry to have laughed like that, my dear," Sebastian Fresh said as he put his arm around Little Lola and led her toward a table where a man wearing a welding mask and some heavy gloves was holding a blow torch. "I know what it's like to be considered **provincial** and it isn't at all nice. In fact, it wasn't until I met Dr. Science that my knowledge of art started to blossom."

"How long have you known Dr. Science?" Lola asked.

"Quite a while, he was one of my mentors," Sebastian responded.

Without saying much more about the history of his relationship with Dr. Science, Sebastian French began to tell Little Lola all about his operations in the tunnel. "You see," he said in a **studious** voice as they watched the man with the blow torch **weld** together two pieces of steel, "art is priceless because the ideas behind it are priceless. And yet, there are a lot of people in the world who pay a lot of money to own the **manifestation** of the idea."

Little Lola looked at Sebastian Fresh with a **flummoxed** look on her face. "What do you mean?"

"A painting is not just a painting, my dear. Before the painting was a painting it was an idea that the artist had **prior** to he or she painting it. The artist's idea behind a piece of art is just as, if not more important than, the actual piece of art."

"Why?" Little Lola asked, still a bit confused.

"Because, my dear, no one else other than the artist had ever had the idea before—it is purely unique."

"So owning a piece of art is like owning an idea?"

"Precisely. And in many cases, these ideas are worth a lot of money."

"But why are some paintings so pretty and some of them are so strange looking? Like that one over there looks so **serene** and peaceful with the trees and the lily pads, but the other one over there with the man holding the head that's been chopped off is so full of **gore**? Shouldn't all of these paintings or ideas be nice ones? Shouldn't they all be beautiful?"

"It isn't necessarily always about beauty, my dear. It is about the idea. After all, beauty comes in **infinite** forms. Where a tree reflected in a stream is beautiful to one artist, a chopped-off head is beautiful to another," Sebastian Fresh answered **astutely**. "Does that make sense?"

"I guess so, but there's something I don't understand," Lola said as she and Sebastian French approached a woman holding a **toxic** spray paint can in each hand.

"Yes?"

"Why are you copying all these paintings and sculptures and stuff? I mean, isn't that like copying or cheating? Doesn't copying it devalue the real piece of art?"

"I have to **commend** you, Lola, on your understanding of what we do here. It isn't often that someone comes to that conclusion so quickly," Sebastian Fresh said trying to avoid answering Little Lola's question.

"But—" Lola said **insistently**.

"I like to think of it more as paying **homage** to the great artists of this world."

"So you're stealing their work and selling fakes to people for the amount of money that they'd pay for the real one."

"Yes, but they're completely **oblivious** about it. If they think it's the real painting, to them it's the real painting and there's no harm done. They are happy because they think they own a priceless sculpture or painting and I am happy because I get their money. Now you must excuse me, my dear. I believe the collection of Matisse paintings has arrived," Sebastian Fresh said as he gallantly showed Little Lola to a comfortable chair near a man who was working on a piece of marble with a **chisel**.

Lola sat down. She needed a little time to consider what all this meant. After all, she didn't really know anything about art and her discussion with Sebastian Fresh was more like a college course than an introduction. Ideas kept swirling through her head. Normally, she wouldn't care if someone was stealing anything. In fact, Little Lola typically thought stealing things was fun, but there was something that didn't sit right with her about stealing someone else's ideas. It was one thing to steal an orange soda or even an emerald, but it was another thing entirely to take someone's hard work and claim it as your own. She remained **sedentary** for quite some time before she finally stood up and walked back over to Dr. Science and Asha Bloom who were in the middle of a rather heated conversation.

"Don't be stupid, Dr. Science, that's like the ugliest painting I've ever seen. I mean, who wants to look at a bunch of dumb cubes and shapes?"

"Asha, you don't understand."

"Um, yes I do. I understand it's not any good."

"You can be so **exasperating** sometimes!"

"Well, at least I'm interested in stuff. You're totally full of **apathy**. I'm surprised you even care about those paintings at all."

"How can you possibly say that when I've devoted my life to paintings like these?"

"Dr. Science, forging paintings and selling them

to idiots doesn't mean you've devoted your life to art, it means you've devoted your life to crime," Asha said while trying to see her reflection in a glass frame. "My hair looks so **luminous** in here."

"It's not your hair, Asha, it's the reflection from all the glass," Dr. Science said coldly as Little Lola smirked.

"Dr. Science, Sebastian said that you were his mentor," Little Lola **intervened** before Asha could come up with a **witty** comeback. "Is that true?"

"Wait a minute, how do you two know each other?" Asha asked. "You'd better tell us exactly what's going on here before Lola and I take The Green Dragon for ourselves."

Sebastian Fresh overheard Asha's threat and joined the group. "Perhaps we should all sit down for some tea and discuss things. It appears as if Dr. Science hasn't been honest with either of us," he said and then snapped his fingers. The tunnel in which we'd all ventured disappeared as the wall moved back into place. We were all trapped. The man with the blow torch looked at all of us with a dangerous gleam in his eye as the woman who had been painting with the two spray paint cans brought us each a cup of tea and some little brown lumps that were supposed to be cookies. They were completely **inedible**.

"So, Dr. Science, it looks as though you have something to share with the rest of us," Sebastian said, glaring at him.

"Well, I, uh…" Dr. Science started to stutter.

"You'd best start from the very beginning. How do

you two know each other?" Asha asked in a demanding voice while Little Lola pulled me onto her lap and tried to feed me one of the disgusting cookies.

As a spy I've been put in plenty **compromising** situations much like the one Dr. Science found himself in with Sebastian Fresh, Asha Bloom, and Little Lola. Obviously he was telling one thing to Sebastian and another thing to Asha and Lola, but who could know which one was the truth? Dr. Science's manner became suddenly **introverted**. You could tell just by looking at him that he was trying to think of a lie to **assuage** everyone. "It seems as if my memory has suffered from some kind of sudden **lapse**."

"Now, now, Dr. Science, don't think that you can get out of the **predicament** you've put yourself in with such a lame excuse," Sebastian said, snapping his fingers. Within seconds the man with the blow torch was standing near the chair Dr. Science was sitting in looking as if he might set Dr. Science's lab coat **aflame**. It was clear from that moment that Dr. Science would not be telling the truth out of his own **volition**, but rather under the threat of four angry peoples' tempers, one of whom was holding a blow torch.

OOOOOOOOOOOO

Dr. Science began his anecdote from when he and Sebastian Fresh first met. It was a few years earlier in autumn. Sebastian was a **docent** at one of the largest museums in New York City. Day in and day out he would walk the galleries and look at famous paintings and warn tourists that they shouldn't get too close to the masterpieces. For Sebastian, it wasn't exactly the greatest job. He saw himself as someone who should be creating art, not guarding it. Every day he grew more and more bitter, that is until he met Dr. Science.

It was a rainy day. Leaves were falling at the same rate as raindrops and Dr. Science had work to do. He sneaked into the museum without paying admission. Somehow he'd lied about having some sort of student identification card that had been stolen, and although the girl selling tickets looked at him with some **scrutiny**, she allowed him into the galleries without **yielding** to her first impression of him, which was that he was most likely there to **transpose** a fake painting for one of the real paintings hanging on the museum walls. Little did she know she was right.

Dr. Science took the escalator to the top floor where the museum displayed its vast collection of paintings, which were **predominantly** from the early 20th century. When he reached the top he took a quick look around to see if there were any guards nearby. Luckily for Dr. Science, the only other person on the floor was Sebastian Fresh, so he calmly started to stroll past the 20th century masters: Pollock, Rothko, Warhol, and others. As Sebastian's footsteps echoed through the **adjacent** gallery, Dr. Science unbuttoned his white lab coat and from within it he pulled out a canvas that looked identical to the one that was hanging in front of him. With no one there to **witness** him, he swapped the fake painting for the real one which he hid quickly inside his lab coat. Just as he'd buttoned the top button and turned to exit the gallery he heard a sigh. It was Sebastian.

"I suppose I should report you to the authorities," Sebastian said quietly.

Not wanting to appear completely guilty Dr. Science tried to make up a believable story. "I'm from downstairs, they told me to replace this painting so we could work on cleaning the real one." His demeanor was **temperate** so as not to cause any unnecessary suspicion.

"Look, I don't really care what you're up to. The fact of the matter is I hate this place. I hate all the faces in the paintings staring at me smugly all day. I hate all abstractions and the theories behind each and every one of these works of so-called art. I don't care if you steal any of them. Take your pick," Sebastian said **virulently** as Dr. Science looked at him a bit surprised.

"But isn't your job to make sure people like me don't come in here and steal paintings?"

"I suppose so, but I really don't care."

From then on Dr. Science and Sebastian had an arrangement: Dr. Science would sneak into the museum with fake paintings in his lab coat and replace the fakes for the real ones, and Sebastian would pretend not to notice. It made Sebastian feel as if he were doing something more exciting than just standing around and telling people not to get too close to the artwork, not to mention it made Dr. Science's job ridiculously easy. Eventually, the two became friends and Dr. Science finally decided to take Sebastian under his wing.

Within a week Sebastian had quit his job at the museum and began to learn everything he could about making reproductions of great masterpieces. Dr. Science was a fantastic teacher. He explained the **discipline** to Sebastian with patience and passion, so much so that it **rekindled** Sebastian's love of art. Unfortunately, his **newfound** passion hadn't been directed in the proper direction and, instead of creating something new and exciting, Sebastian found himself copying a **medley** of masterpieces for Dr. Science. One week he would find himself working on some impressionistic paintings and the next week he'd be working on Grecian marble sculptures. Each and every time he copied a masterpiece, Sebastian got a sense of revenge which eventually took over his good nature. In the meantime, Dr. Science was stealing pieces of art from all over the world and although no one was aware of what was going on it was causing **irreparable** damage to museums and art collectors **alike**.

But as all criminals do, Dr. Science got bored with just making reproductions of masterpieces and stealing them. He wanted something to offer him a greater challenge, so he left the counterfeiting to his greatest apprentice, Sebastian Fresh, and went out in search of a greater challenge. This is how he met Asha Bloom.

Asha, as we know, was a notorious jewel thief and through various contacts and connections Dr. Science met her one day on ferry boat in the Greek Islands. Dr. Science managed to **extract** all the knowledge she had about The Green Dragon from her and promised her that he would help her steal it. He, however, hadn't been completely **upfront** with Asha when they first discussed stealing the mysterious jewel. Asha had paid him to help her. Although Dr. Science took her money and told her he'd do as she wished, he had other plans—plans that involved Sebastian Fresh and his collection of stolen paintings.

OOOOOOOOOOO

"So what's the grand plan then, Dr. Science?" Asha asked in a betrayed sort of tone.

"Look, we don't have to give up either of your plans," Dr. Science explained. "Sebastian, we can still use The Green Dragon at the Louvre like we'd planned and when we're finished with it you can have it."

"What do you mean 'use it at the Louvre'?" Asha asked.

"We were planning on using The Green Dragon to hypnotize the visitors, the guards, and the staff at the Louvre so that we can steal and replace their entire art collection," Sebastian admitted.

"What? Don't you think that's a bit **risqué,** not to mention entirely stupid?" Asha asked. "I mean, you'd get caught instantly. There'd be **warrants** out for your arrest in every single country in the entire world."

"That's the point of having The Green Dragon, Asha. No one would know that any of the sculptures or paintings had been replaced because they'd all be hypnotized," Dr. Science explained and took a brief **reprieve** from talking to sip from his cold cup of tea.

Asha shot Dr. Science a furious look. After all, she had been betrayed by him. He was going to give her a copy of The Green Dragon and use the real one for himself. She sat and weighed her options. She could either help Dr. Science and keep the real Green Dragon and take a cut from the **proceeds** from the stolen artwork, or she could just leave with the real Green Dragon. She decided that the first option was slightly more agreeable and said, "I want in on the cut."

Sebastian Fresh and Dr. Science looked at each other and excused themselves to talk things over. They returned quite quickly to **resume** their discussion and negotiations involving their upcoming **heist**. **Unanimously**, they decided that it would be more **beneficial** for Asha to be in on the cut.

All three of them felt a new sense of **wellbeing**. Not only would they have the power of The Green Dragon behind them, but they'd also soon be incredibly rich from selling off stolen, original pieces from the **Mecca** of masterpieces: the Louvre in Paris. This sense of **camaraderie** was a **novel** concept to all three of them. They were so used to being selfish and backstabbing that it actually felt good to be part of a team. Unfortunately, it was much too late when they realized that one of their supposed team members had run away. And she'd run away with The Green Dragon safely tucked underneath her favorite cap.

Little Lola had had enough. She tried her hardest to stay in a good mood while Dr. Science, Asha Bloom, and Sebastian Fresh sat around and made plans to break into the Louvre, but as they forgot to include her in these plans she **succumbed** to feeling more and more down in the dumps. She didn't want the **pittance** they were most likely going to offer her for The Green Dragon. She didn't think it was at all fair. After all, she was the one who was clever enough to snatch it out of Candy Cottonshank's purse and she was the one who had been carrying it around uncomfortably in her cap this whole time. Dr. Science and Asha didn't even treat her as a **relevant** part of their criminal crew. All they wanted was someone who would **comply** with their dumb schemes, and Little Lola was sick and tired of being that someone.

Watching Asha and Sebastian Fresh **fawn** over Dr. Science as he began to **orate** his plans for breaking into the Louvre was the last straw. Little Lola didn't feel included at all, so **solemnly** she sneaked away towards one of the rock walls and found a small hole large enough to push me through and then wiggle through herself. "They'll miss me once they know I've left with their precious emerald," she said as we began our **descent** back toward the doors that greeted us upon falling into the lagoon.

"I'm sick of being treated like I'm **obsolete** and unimportant. Asha and her stupid hairdo and Dr. Science and his dumb lab coat—they'll be sorry once they haven't got me to push around any longer. And that

Sebastian Fresh, he's some kind of **enigma**. He didn't even make any sense with all that talk about art and ideas. What's he getting at anyhow? Sometimes a painting is just a great painting and people like it because it's beautiful, not because it's some kind of crazy idea." Little Lola continued to **declaim** Dr. Science, Asha, and Sebastian Fresh while she carried me to the doors that presumably led somewhere other than the cave in which Sebastian kept all his stolen artwork. When we finally arrived she marched straight over to the door with splotches on it and said, "Yup, I bet I've caused them some kind of **crisis** now that The Green Dragon isn't near, but I don't even care. They can't have it. I can go to Paris by myself." And with that she turned the large colorful doorknob and we found ourselves in a **diverse** tunnel from the one we'd found ourselves in before.

Once Little Lola had shut the door behind her we heard an incredibly loud whistle and saw some very bright lights speeding toward us. It took mere seconds for me to figure out that it was a train. Somehow Lola and I had entered into a sort of subway system. From the look on Lola's face you could tell she thought that the train was quite **expedient**, if not a little **fortuitous**. "You see, kitty, it's meant to be! We wanted to leave and here's a train coming to take us away." I, of course, didn't feel the same way about the train that Lola did, but as it was my duty to follow The Green Dragon, I was forced to stay with her and board the train.

We quickly jumped on to one of the cars as the train jerked to a stop at the platform. All the seats on board were completely empty and one of the overhead lights had gone out giving the car a slightly **ominous** appearance. We sat down near a window and the voice of the train conductor shouted, "Next stop, Paris!"

○○○○○○○○○○○○○

"Where on earth could she have gone?" Dr. Science screamed in a panic, accidentally knocking over a rather **potent**-smelling can of red paint.

In a **similar** fashion, Asha looked around the room, bumping into replicas of different art works calling out Lola's name, "Lola, Lola, where are you? This isn't funny anymore. Come out right now!"

"Forgive me for **broaching** such a sensitive topic, but what does it matter if that stupid little girl ran off?" Sebastian Fresh asked as he tried to protect a **gilded** frame from Asha's rampage.

"She has The Green Dragon," Dr. Science answered simply.

Sebastian's jaw almost dropped to the floor. "What do you mean she has The Green Dragon?"

Dr. Science offered Sebastian a **cursory** version of how Little Lola had stolen the emerald from Candy Cottonshank's purse. It wasn't the whole story, but it was enough for him to understand what had happened up until they'd all reached the tunnel.

"Congratulations are in order, it seems," Sebastian said, starting to applaud sarcastically. "I have to offer both of you **kudos** for being the biggest idiots in the world."

"Idiots? How dare you call us idiots?" Asha Bloom said, taking great offense.

"How dare I? Well, let's see, as far as I can **surmise**, the two of you pushed Little Lola away by treating her poorly, thus losing The Green Dragon again. If that isn't idiotic, I don't know what is."

"Sebastian is right, Asha," Dr. Science said. "We should have been more concerned with how Lola would react. But instead of fighting amongst ourselves now, we've got to find out where she's gone. We need a new plan. Now, what **pertinent** information do we know about Little Lola that will help us find her and recover The Green Dragon?"

"She has that stupid cat with her," Asha said flopping down into an overstuffed chair and sulking because instead of paying attention to her, now Dr. Science and Sebastian Fresh were more concerned with Little Lola.

"I don't think the cat is at all significant. I mean, other than keeping her company, what can a cat do? It's not like a cat knows kung-fu or how to bake a soufflé," Sebastian observed.

"Yes, what else do we know about Lola?" Dr. Science said, thinking out loud.

"She loves orange soda," Asha said.

"Good, good. That sort of information will help us in the long run."

"Look," Sebastian Fresh suddenly called out. "There's been a **breach** in the train tunnel."

"The train tunnel?" Asha asked him trying to understand what he meant.

Sebastian laughed a little before he answered her.

"Before we made these tunnels our headquarters they were used **explicitly** for underground trains that were **abandoned** ages ago. I cleverly decided to keep one of the trains that heads straight for Paris so that I could transport the stolen art more easily. Each of the doors at the entrance to our headquarters leads to something else. One leads to our cave, one leads to the train…"

Before he could finish telling where the other tunnels led to Dr. Science interrupted him. "Sebastian, which door leads to the train tunnel?"

"The door with the splotches."

"That was Lola's favorite door!" Asha exclaimed.

"Yes, that's it. She must have gone through the door and gotten on the train," Dr. Science said.

"Which means she'll arrive in Paris in a few hours," Sebastian added.

"It's **imperative** that we think and act quickly," Dr. Science pointed out as he **paced** back and forth.

Asha was nervous and started to **gorge** herself on the plate of disgusting cookies that had been sitting there since Little Lola left. "We just have to find her. That's all there is to it," she said.

"But how are we supposed to find her in a city as big as Paris? And what exactly do you suggest we do once we do find her? It's obvious that we can't just go up to her and make nice," Sebastian stated, joining Dr. Science in his pacing.

"I think I've got a plan," Dr. Science finally said.

"I'm not sure we should trust your plans anymore, Dr. Science. They've gotten us into mess after mess without **exception**," Asha said with her mouth full.

"Trust me, Asha, this plan is very simple. Little Lola will most likely be **downtrodden** and upset when she reaches Paris, so the first thing she'll do is try to cheer herself up with an orange soda."

"One of the few soda fountains in Paris is very near where the train stops in Paris," Sebastian said nodding.

"Lola will most likely stop for an orange soda. In fact, she'll probably drink more than one. In the meantime, one of us will disguise ourselves as a nice French lady who will offer to take care of her."

"And then what?" Asha asked.

"Well, then we kidnap her, of course," answered Dr. Science.

"That's the dumbest plan I've ever heard," Asha said. "Little Lola never talks to strangers."

"Have you got a better idea?" Sebastian asked. Asha shook her head.

"All right then, we've got to get to Paris and quickly. There's no telling how long Lola will sit at that soda fountain drinking orange sodas. We haven't got any time to lose," said Dr. Science as he shoved something into the inside pocket of his white lab coat.

"Follow me," Sebastian said. "We can take my jet."

Both Dr. Science and Asha looked at Sebastian Fresh as if her were some kind of **prodigal** art thief. "You have a jet? Isn't that kind of expensive?" Dr. Science asked.

Sebastian Fresh just smiled and snapped his fingers and before too long the three of them had entered the jewel-encrusted door and were boarding his private jet.

True or False

Decide whether the following statements are True or False about Chapter 1. If the statement is true, write a "T" next to it. If the statement is false, write an "F" next to it.

1. Dr. Science's memory lapsed when he was forced to tell the truth about how he knew Sebastian Fresh.
2. It isn't a crisis for Dr. Science, Asha Bloom and Sebastian Fresh when Little Lola and The Cat run away to Paris.
3. It is a unanimous decision between The Cat and Little Lola to get on the train and travel back to Dublin.
4. Dr. Science offers Sebastian Fresh kudos on creating such practical headquarters.
5. Dr. Science and Sebastian Fresh find themselves in a quandary when Little Lola runs away.
6. Sebastian Fresh has cursory knowledge of how Little Lola got The Green Dragon.
7. Upon entering the tunnel Little Lola, Asha, and Dr. Science are threatened with psychological and physical damage.
8. Many of the chemicals in Sebastian Fresh's headquarters are toxic.

9. Little Lola doesn't cause irreparable damage to Dr. Science's plan when she decides to run away.

10. Knowing that she has The Green Dragon under her cap helps Little Lola's mood convalesce and get better.

11. Dr. Science undergoes a great amount of trauma when he has to tell the truth about his past.

12. Little Lola isn't considered provincial by her so-called friends.

13. It's irrelevant to know that Little Lola loves orange soda.

14. Sebastian Fresh commends Little Lola's quick understanding of his theories of art.

15. When he steals works of art, Sebastian Fresh does not like to transpose fake replicas in exchange for the real masterpieces.

16. Asha Bloom has a prodigal attitude towards jewels.

17. Sebastian Fresh's personality is very introverted.

18. Little Lola runs away because she does not want to comply with Dr. Science's plan to break into The Louvre in Paris.

19. Prior to working with Asha Bloom, Dr. Science was Sebastian Fresh's mentor.

20. The Cat tries to intervene when Little Lola decides to run away.

21. Asha Bloom tries to procrastinate before they board Sebastian Fresh's private jet.

22. Sebastian Fresh's headquarters has a huge capacity to hold stolen art work.
23. The Cat's temper is very temperate.
24. Dr. Science interrogates Sebastian about Little Lola's likes and dislikes.
25. It is hard for Sebastian Fresh to broach the topic of stealing works of art from The Louvre.

Relationships

Decide what type of relationship the words below have to each other. If the words have similar meanings, write "S" next to the pair of words. If they have different or opposite meanings, write "O" next to the words.

1. synthetic :: real
2. predominant :: minor
3. inedible :: delicious
4. succumb :: surrender
5. pragmatic :: impractical
6. hysterical :: agitated
7. potent :: strong-smelling
8. astute :: unintelligent

9. homage :: honor
10. studious :: careless
11. pompous :: humble
12. anticipate :: expect
13. gore :: clean
14. apathy :: passion
15. plea :: request
16. solemn :: excited
17. pittance :: ration
18. gorge :: starve
19. pitch :: light
20. skeptic :: believer
21. placate :: soothe
22. gallant :: cowardly
23. similar :: opposite
24. pertinent :: important
25. gallows :: hanging grounds
26. scrutiny :: close examination
27. pathological :: diseased
28. pry :: mind your own business

Fill in the Blank

Choose the word that best completes each of the following sentences.

1. Michelle left the movie of her own _____ because it was boring.

   a. accord

   b. volition

   c. desire

   d. need

2. Brian was hoping for a short _____ between his two most difficult classes at school.

   a. nap

   b. lunch

   c. reprieve

   d. postponement

3. William had a _____ idea when he invented a toilet that cleaned itself.

    a. bland

    b. mediocre

    c. smart

    d. novel

4. The disappearance of Robert's pet hamster was quite a/an _____.

    a. enigma

    b. event

    c. tragedy

    d. problem

5. Sean's criticism of his best friend Tyler was rather _____ during their fight.

    a. harsh

    b. virulent

    c. infectious

    d. grand

6. Judy liked it when her grandparents would sit on their front porch and _____ about when they were children.

   a. talk

   b. think

   c. laugh

   d. reminisce

7. New York City is often a/an _____ for tourists from around the world.

   a. mecca

   b. intention

   c. plan

   d. goal

8. It's a good thing to be interested in _____ activities.

   a. some

   b. prior

   c. diverse

   d. potent

9. Natasha was caught _____ her school locker and had to go to detention.

   a. stealing

   b. cleaning

   c. breaking

   d. vandalizing

10. Marla was _____ to go to the hospital even though she needed to get stitches.

    a. reluctant

    b. excited

    c. frustrated

    d. bored

11. Brad thought that it was a good idea to bring a _____ of fruit home to his grandmother instead of just apples.

    a. jumble

    b. medley

    c. pittance

    d. bouquet

12. Edward _____ between buying a bagel or a sandwich for lunch.

   a. decided

   b. thought

   c. vacillated

   d. fought

13. Lou felt very smart after he made a very _____ point during his math class.

   a. funny

   b. selected

   c. nice

   d. relevant

14. Harriet was disgusted when she read about the _____ mobs that were common in the Southern United States before the Civil War.

   a. frightening

   b. lynch

   c. racist

   d. angry

15. Danny chose engineering as the _____
he wanted to study in college.

    a. area

    b. idea

    c. discipline

    d. issue

16. In order for the police to search your house
they must first have a _____.

    a. permission

    b. note

    c. letter

    d. warrant

17. Max took _____ in the fact that he
was right about quitting his job.

    a. refuge

    b. comfort

    c. peace

    d. anxiety

18. Annie was amazed at how _____ the collection of stain glass windows were at the museum.

    a. unattractive

    b. pretty

    c. luminous

    d. pertinent

19. Before they made their _____ into the mouth of the cave Julie and Sam thought it would be a good idea to make sure their flashlight worked.

    a. way

    b. descent

    c. homage

    d. steps

20. If you _____ a crime take place it's best to call the police immediately.

    a. notice

    b. see

    c. participate

    d. witness

21. Jill decided to _____ her differences with Amy.

    a. pretend

    b. reconcile

    c. refuge

    d. discuss

22. Carrie was relieved that the principal was _____ with her even though she'd broken the school rules.

    a. compassionate

    b. irreparable

    c. prodigal

    d. lenient

23. Susan felt a sense of _____ after she'd had a fight with her mom.

    a. dejection

    b. fickleness

    c. passion

    d. sorrow

24. When you're riding your bike it is always wise to _____ to pedestrians.

a. stop

b. wave

c. yield

d. salute

25. As an excellent student, Melanie had a certain _____ with all of her teachers.

a. attitude

b. expedient

c. scrutiny

d. rapport

Matching

Match each word on the left to a word with the similar meaning on the right.

1. sedentary   a. useful
2. ostracize   b. strategy
3. explicit   c. harsh
4. underfoot   d. impose
5. severe   e. confused
6. orate   f. continue
7. expedient   g. bind
8. inclination   h. unlimited
9. risqué   i. specific
10. obtrusive   j. harmony
11. exception   k. demanding
12. rant   l. dangerous
13. resume   m. actualization
14. obsolete   n. speak
15. euphony   o. tool
16. tactic   p. nosy
17. realistically   q. tease
18. oblivious   r. tendency
19. inflict   s. underneath
20. weld   t. sensibly
21. manifestation   u. tirade
22. flummoxed   v. unused
23. infinite   w. motionless
24. insistent   x. unaware
25. chisel   y. abnormality

Relationships

Decide what type of relationship the words below have to each other. If the words have similar meanings, write "S" next to the pair of words. If they have different or opposite meanings, write "O" next to the words.

1. exasperating :: annoying
2. witty :: funny
3. compromising :: comfortable
4. assuage :: aggravate
5. predicament :: trouble
6. aflame :: blazing
7. docent :: guide
8. adjacent :: distant
9. rekindle :: restart
10. newfound :: discovered
11. alike :: different
12. upfront :: dishonest
13. extract :: remove
14. proceeds :: losses
15. comradery :: enemies
16. wellbeing :: discomfort
17. heist :: robbery
18. beneficial :: disadvantageous
19. fawn :: ignore
20. declaim :: denounce
21. fortuitous :: lucky
22. ominous :: promising

23. gilded :: golden
24. surmise :: guess
25. abandoned :: used
26. breach :: violation
27. imperative :: unimportant
28. pace :: walk
29. downtrodden :: satisfied

CHAPTER 8

From Paris With Love

Ah, Paris, the city of lights. It's such a spectacular and romantic place. There's a wide **array** of things to do. You can go to one of the many famous art museums or one of the perfectly **manicured** parks. You can **gallivant** from one **lavish** café to the next drinking ridiculously strong coffee in small cups. You can eat stacks and stacks of delicious **crêpes**. You can visit the **immaculate** shops that sell **vivid** scarves and **impractical** handbags. You can go to an old movie theater and watch a dramatic French film from start to **climax**, or go to the opera and watch one of the poor characters sing bravely though they are **condemned** to death. This is just barely **skimming** the surface of the pleasures Paris has to offer its visitors. It's absolutely impossible to be bored in Paris, unless you find yourself sitting at a soda fountain with Little Lola who has decided to deplete the town of its supply of orange soda.

I've been faced with several different situations where I thought that I might **divulge** my true identity. As I sat next to Little Lola, who was mumbling things into her straw, I wondered whether I should tell her that I was not a cat and that I was, in fact, a spy. Of course, I had been trained to **persevere** and no matter how **disparaging** a situation got, I was supposed to remain undercover. Yet something about the mess we were in now told me that it might be wise to stop **concealing** my true self. If I could talk to Lola instead of just meow I might be able help her. I could explain that her **fidelity** to Dr. Science and Asha Bloom was **futile** and that no matter what, they'd always **discount** her. They would always be right and she would always be wrong. They would always be smarter and better at everything and she would always be subject to their manipulations. If I talked to her about all this, I might be able to convince her that they were **heathens** and bad friends. And I might be able to **persuade** her to give up The Green Dragon so that I could destroy it. But before I could **utter** one **syllable**, a woman in a **tartan** skirt approached Little Lola and began to talk to her.

"Are you lost, little girl?" the woman asked Little Lola.

I could tell immediately that something wasn't quite right with the woman in the tartan skirt. Firstly, her accent was **indecipherable**. It sounded as if she was trying to fake an English accent, but there was a hint of Swedish, French, Irish, American, and perhaps an **indefinite** amount of Japanese mixed in with the sound of her voice. She was also wearing far too much makeup. Perhaps I'm **discriminating** a tad, but I don't know many older women who wear glitter eye shadow and bubblegum pink **rouge**. And finally, her stockings weren't **identical**. One of them was orange and the other was green. In my experience, most people wear matching socks. In fact, I find socks to be rather **generic** in general. Either this woman was completely color blind or she had some other **objective** in mind and didn't have very much time to get dressed before she met it.

Little Lola looked up from her glass of orange soda and looked from the top of the woman's head to the tips of her toes. Obviously, Lola didn't have the same sort of **bias** that I did. I even think that Lola actually liked the fact that the woman's stockings didn't match.

"I guess I'm kind of lost," Lola finally answered. "I mean, I know I'm in Paris, but I don't really know where in Paris I am. It's so confusing."

"There, there, my pet," the woman in the tartan skirt **cooed** putting her arm around Lola **sympathetically**. "Don't you worry about a thing. Mrs. Nanpants will take good care of you."

"Who is Mrs. Nanpants?" Lola asked backing away a bit.

"Why, I'm Mrs. Nanpants," the woman in the tartan skirt replied. "And I'm going to make sure you're looked after."

"I'm not sure that I really need looking after," Lola said.

"Don't be such a silly, little goose," Mrs. Nanpants said grabbing Little Lola's wrist and yanking her to her feet. "All lost little girls need looking after."

"Look, I'm not a little girl and I'm not that lost," Lola argued, but Mrs. Nanpants wouldn't hear it. Nor would she **relinquish** the tight grip she had on Little Lola's wrist. "Let go of me!" Lola yelled as **passersby** tried to mind their own business.

I didn't know quite what to do, I could try to scratch Mrs. Nanpants' **outlandish** stockings to help Little Lola get free, but if I did that Lola and I would just be in the same situation we were before, **stagnantly** sitting at a soda fountain staring at empty glasses of orange soda. Lola was, after all, **relentless** about her **consumption** of orange soda. In this situation I thought it best to rely on my training. As a spy the first thing you're taught is to be a good **observer**. It was clear that I'd do far better observing what was happening than **participating** in it. I could help Little Lola later.

As it happened, my suspicions were correct: Mrs. Nanpants did have something **nefarious** up her old lady sleeves. Lola squirmed and wiggled with all of her might, but she was no match for Mrs. Nanpants who had managed to drag her from the soda fountain to the sidewalk where Lola was trying to kick her in the shin.

"HELP ME! HELP!" Lola screamed, but no one seemed to be paying any attention to her. Mrs. Nanpants mumbled something in French and the passing people just shook their heads. Finally, as Mrs. Nanpants was trying to shove Lola into the trunk of her car, a man carrying a load of packages and books asked if everything was all right.

"Is everything all right here?" the man carrying the load of packages and books asked.

"Of course, of course, I just have a naughty little girl on my hands who doesn't seem to want to leave the soda fountain. You know how it is," Mrs. Nanpants answered in a voice as sweet as one of Lola's favorite orange **libations**.

"Don't listen to her! Help me, help me," Lola shouted as the man smiled.

"You should listen to your mother, little girl," the man said, **adjusting** the weight of his packages and books from one arm to the other. "You don't want to get in trouble when you get home, do you?"

"But she's not my mother," Lola cried and tried to squirm away as Mrs. Nanpants gave her a kiss on the cheek.

"Now you be a good little girl and get in the car," Mrs. Nanpants said roughly shoving Lola into the trunk with one hand and waving **adieu** to the man with the load of packages and books with the other.

As Mrs. Nanpants quickly got behind the wheel of her rusty old car and started the engine, I hopped up onto the roof and held on for dear life. Mrs. Nanpants might have been good at kidnapping, but she was a terrible driver. She sped away from the scene of the soda fountain as fast as she possibly could. It was as if she was **emulating** some kind of racecar driver and although she kept telling Lola to be quiet you could still hear Lola in the trunk kicking and shouting to be **liberated**.

oooooooooooo

"I just don't know, Dr. Science, Lola isn't a complete idiot. I don't think she'll fall for Mrs. Nanpants," Asha said, looking out the window to see if the old lady's car was approaching their new hideout.

"Look," Sebastian French interjected before Dr. Science could say anything, "Mrs. Nanpants is a professional. If she doesn't get the job done no one can. I've used her for jobs time and time again."

"Although her **employment** may have **recurred** with you, Sebastian, Asha and I have no reason to trust her. She seemed a bit loony to me," Dr. Science finally said.

"Well, it wasn't my plan to kidnap her," Sebastian Fresh said with a slight hint of **animosity** in his voice.

"Kidnapping her was the only thing I could think of on such short notice. It was the quickest way to get Lola and The Green Dragon back to us," Dr. Science said trying to defend his **unscrupulous** plan. "If the plan doesn't work it isn't my fault. It's that **menace**, Mrs. Nanpants. I don't think she's a professional at all. She's just a **hapless** old lady out to cause trouble."

"Did you get a look at those **repulsive** stockings she was wearing? Lola would never get into a car with someone wearing those things, let alone that **unsightly** tartan skirt. I mean, seriously, who wears plaid anymore?" Asha observed while still anxiously watching for Mrs. Nanpants' car arrive. Although she was trying to act cool and **unconcerned**, Asha was actually worried about her friend, Little Lola. She knew that she didn't always treat Lola with a lot of respect and that it may have **tarnished** their friendship, but when she saw Lola again, she had resolved to make things right. Asha was even prepared to supply Little Lola with gallons and gallons of orange soda if that is what it would take to **appease** her.

"Her stockings were rather strange," Dr. Science admitted and went to look out the window with Asha.

"If it weren't for me hiring Mrs. Nanpants in the first place, you two **hypocrites** wouldn't even see Little Lola again, so I don't want to hear anymore of your **gibberish** or whining. I'll bet that Mrs. Nanpants already has Lola tied up in the trunk of her car."

"You'd better be right, Sebastian. If this doesn't work none of us will see The Green Dragon or Lola again," Dr. Science said.

Fortunately for the three of them, Mrs. Nanpants's car suddenly came into view with me holding onto the roof for my life. It would have been far more practical of me to jump into the back seat of the car or even into the trunk with Little Lola, but sometimes one doesn't think of these things until they're holding onto the top of a car for dear life while a madwoman speeds to an **undisclosed** location. Mrs. Nanpants honked her horn three times and a large door opened up so that she could drive through it. When the door closed behind her she got out of the car and dusted off her tartan skirt. "Oh dear, oh dear, that little brat made me get a hole in my favorite stockings. You'll owe me extra for that, Mr. Fresh."

"But of course, Mrs. Nanpants. We wouldn't dream of **depriving** you of your fashionable choice in **hosiery**. But before we settle over your stockings where is the little brat? I mean, where is our dear lost Little Lola? We've been worried sick."

"I'm in here," came a voice from the trunk. "And you'd better let me out!"

"It seems as if she doesn't really like the trunk," Mrs. Nanpants said.

"Well, none of us really do, now do we, Mrs. Nanpants? Being locked in a trunk does seem to **exacerbate** someone's temper. Why don't we let her out?" Sebastian Fresh said trying to **augment** both Mrs. Nanpants's and Little Lola's moods.

"Oh all right, but she'd better apologize for ruining my favorite pair of stockings," Mrs. Nanpants said

begrudgingly as she unlocked the trunk of her car. Little Lola flew out of the car in an absolute rage. I'd never seen anyone so angry before. It was as if she were trying to **vanquish** all the bad things that had ever happened to her all at once.

As soon as she was out of the trunk, Little Lola shoved Mrs. Nanpants to the ground and kicked her in the shins. "There, that's what I think of your dumb stockings, lady!" Then she moved toward Sebastian Fresh and gave him a black eye. Dr. Science and Asha Bloom backed away from her to try to **evade** her temper, but they weren't fast enough. Lola swooped down upon Asha Bloom and yanked her sunglasses from her face. Then, she threw them on the ground and in one stomp completely **obliterated** them. After she was finished with Asha, she moved toward Dr. Science. Quickly she grabbed a can of spray paint that was lying on the ground and sprayed red polka-dots all over his **pristine** lab coat.

After her tantrum had **subsided** a little Asha finally spoke. "Lola, I know we all may have deserved that, but we want you to know that we're sorry."

"I don't care if you're sorry," Lola said, trying not to cry. Even I, the toughest of spies disguised as a cat, felt sorry for her. It wasn't on her **agenda** to use The Green Dragon to steal paintings from the most famous art museum in the world, nor was it her idea to use the emerald to decorate a lousy pair of sunglasses. She'd just come along for the adventure and now she'd wound up kidnapped by a crazy old lady in a tartan skirt and ugly stockings and couldn't trust any of her so-called friends. Given the situation, anyone would be **vexed**.

"We haven't got time for this," Dr. Science said as Little Lola sulked.

"Dr. Science, don't be such a jerk. We all owe Lola an apology," Asha said.

"Since when are you an **advocate** for apologies, Asha?" Dr. Science **quibbled**.

Sensing that he might have more to gain by being nice Sebastian Fresh joined Asha and apologized to Little Lola.

"I'm terribly sorry we've offended you, Lola. If there's anything we can do to put this **affront** behind us, please let us know," Sebastian said in a rather formal and insincere manner.

"I'm sorry too, Lola. I shouldn't have gotten you into this scheme. It's just that I thought it would be fun and I really wanted The Green Dragon for my sunglasses," Asha added, clearing her throat to give a signal to Dr. Science that he should apologize as well.

"Oh, all right, I'm sorry too," Dr. Science said.

"Well, I don't care about any of you," Mrs. Nanpants interrupted. "My stockings are ruined and my shins are bruised. And I'm not sure what this Green Dragon thing is, but it doesn't sound worth the trouble if you ask me."

"Shut up, you old hag," Lola shouted at her.

Sebastian could tell that Mrs. Nanpants was the one who was more trouble than she was worth. He'd told her that she should be sweet to Little Lola, not to throw her in the trunk of a car. If Mrs. Nanpants had done as she was instructed they wouldn't be in this mess. But instead of fighting with her, he just gave her the money she was promised as well as a little extra so that she could buy a new pair of hideous stockings.

"Thank you for your help, Mrs. Nanpants," he said quietly escorting her to the door. She went along with him and stormed off in a **huff**, completely forgetting that she'd left her beat-up old car in their hideout.

As Sebastian closed the door behind him he noticed me hiding behind one of the tires observing the goings-on. "Well, well, well," he said, "look what I've found." He quickly picked me up and brought me over to Lola. And here I thought that I'd be able to go back to being a spy rather than a pet, but it seems that I was going to have to do both if I wanted to get my paws on The Green Dragon, because even after all the **chaos** it was still safely tucked underneath Lola's cap.

"We can't just sit here all day and stroke cats," Dr. Science said trying to scrub the red polka-dots out of his lab coat with a strange **vial** of liquid he'd taken from one of its pockets. "We've got a lot of planning to do if we're going to break into the Louvre tomorrow."

"Dr. Science is right," Asha agreed.

"But Asha, you only wanted The Green Dragon for you sunglasses," Lola said. "Why do you want to break into the museum?"

"Lola, if we break into the museum and steal all the artwork with Sebastian and Dr. Science I'll eventu-ally be able to get as many pairs of fancy sunglasses as I want. Just think of it, I'll have loads of fantastic outfits and sunglasses and you can have all the orange soda you've ever dreamed of."

Lola sat for a minute to consider what Asha had suggested. Not only could she have all the orange soda she'd ever wanted, but she could probably have anything else she ever wanted too. "I guess you're right, Asha."

"So you're with us then?" Sebastian asked.

"I guess I'm with you, but on one condition."

"What's that, Lola?" Asha asked.

"I get to be in charge of The Green Dragon."

"That's fine with me," Asha said.

"Me, too," agreed Sebastian.

"Oh, all right," Dr. Science finally added. "You can be in charge of The Green Dragon."

OOOOOOOOOOOO

The Louvre in Paris is one of the biggest museums in the entire world. It's very easy to get lost inside. You could almost certainly spend days and days looking at the huge collection of art and antiques, which is most likely why Dr. Science, Asha Bloom, and Little Lola were feeling a bit **daunted** as they waited on the steps the next morning while Sebastian Fresh went to purchase **admission** tickets.

"Tell me why we have to get tickets again?" Asha asked.

"We don't want to arouse suspicion before we get inside, Asha, I've told you again and again. Now stick to the plan, will you," an irritated Dr. Science said.

"Well, I don't see why we can't just use The Green Dragon now?" Asha said back.

"Because that's not the plan," Dr. Science said, growing even more impatient.

"Can I trade collections with you?" Little Lola chimed in. "It's just that I'm not really interested in Decorative Arts, I'd much rather steal paintings."

"Stop trying to change the plan, you two," Dr. Science said, obviously fed up with both of them. "You stick to Decorative Arts, Asha will stay with paintings."

"But—" Lola tried to argue.

"No, buts! We're not going to change the plan."

Just then Sebastian Fresh came toward us holding tickets and maps in different languages. "Look," he said, "They print the maps in loads of different languages and these little pictures **depict** where there's a cafeteria or shops or bathrooms. Isn't that just fantastic?" he said excitedly.

"Sebastian, we don't need maps in other languages. Now give Asha and Lola their tickets so they can get started with the plan."

"Fine," Sebastian said and started handing out the passes to get into the museum. "But there's one little problem."

"Of course there is," Dr. Science said. "Go on, what is it?"

"The cat is **inadmissible**."

"What," Lola asked getting upset.

"No pets allowed," Sebastian told her. "It cleverly says so in many different languages on the map I just gave you. It even has that little picture with a slash going through the kitten to say that you can't bring pets into the museum."

"No cat, no Lola," Little Lola said and planted herself back on one of the steps.

"Oh, come on, Lola, the cat will be waiting for you out here when we're finished. If you want we can even put him in the truck out back where we're going to load the art," Dr. Science said in his most convincing voice.

"But I don't feel safe without him," Lola said.

"No pets," Sebastian pointed out again.

"OK! OK! I get it, no pets," Lola said as Asha ignored the whole argument and applied some new lipstick to her lips. Lola stood up and put me back down on the step. "You be a good kitty and wait for me. I'll be back very soon," she said patting me on the head.

It was my lucky break. As the four of them walked toward the entrance, I scurried off. I had plans of my own involving The Green Dragon.

OOOOOOOOOOOO

Being a security guard isn't that much different than being a spy. Both require being **apt** at observation, only security guards have uniforms and keep watch over things so they don't get damaged or stolen and spies wear disguises and keep watch over criminals. This is most likely why it was so easy for me to sneak into the security guards' break room and swap my cat disguise for one of their uniforms.

Just as I had finished tying the rather **dapper** necktie that the uniform required two young security guards came into the break room practically ready to burst with laughter. One of their nametags read "AIDAN," and the other read "IAN."

"Stop **gloating** so much, you always get to see way crazier stuff when you're guarding the paintings than you do when you're guarding Decorative Arts," the one with the nametag that read "AIDAN" said, trying to hold in a giggle.

"I can't help it. It was just too funny. Who **smuggles** a parrot into a museum and then tries to teach it the names of all the paintings? Seriously, who does that?" the guard with the nametag that read "IAN" said.

"Maybe it was a pirate with a love of art. In any case, that's pretty funny," Aidan said.

"What was funniest was that the parrot kept screwing up all the names and then it would get more and more frustrated and ask the paintings if they wanted a cracker."

"Painting want a cracker?" Aidan said, imitating a parrot and both of them started laughing again.

"Hey, are you new on the job?" one of them asked, finally noticing that I was in the break room.

"Yes, yes I am. It's my first day," I said **fiddling** with one of the buttons on the **blazer** I was required to wear.

"I'm Ian and this is Aidan. We're exchange students from America," Ian said offering me his hand. As we shook hands Aidan came over and offered his hand next. They seemed to be very pleasant security guards. "We just stopped in for a quick bite to eat and then we've got to get back to our posts. Would you like to share some lunch?"

"That's very generous of you," I said, taking a tuna fish sandwich.

The three of us shared their lunch and Aidan and Ian told me stories about guarding the different parts of the museum. Aidan swore than the Egyptian wing was haunted by an angry mummy. Ian told me a story about a time when a bunch of witches tried to do a magic spell on one of the sculptures to bring it to life. It was plain to see that both Aidan and Ian liked their jobs and liked being exchange students from America. I could tell that I could trust both of them and felt like I should tell them what was going to happen. I tried not to be too **verbose** in telling them the whole account of how Little Lola had obtained The Green Dragon. Both Aidan and Ian thought the story about King Bruce and the peanut butter was hilarious and, although they couldn't quite **fathom** how important it was to get the emerald out of the wrong hands, they **pledged** that they would try to help me if they could. I also told them the secret words to be repeated so as not to be hypnotized by The Green Dragon. I know the words were dangerous to give away, but I would need allies if I wanted to destroy that menacing jewel for good.

"Ian, look at the time, we've got to hurry," Aidan said shoving the last sandwich in his mouth.

"We have to get back to our posts now. Don't worry, if we see your Green Dragon, we'll help you get it back," Ian said, dusting the crumbs off of his uniform. And then as quickly as they'd come into the break room, they left to go back to their posts.

I needed to hurry as well. Dr. Science, Asha Bloom, Little Lola, and Sebastian Fresh were most likely almost through the line to get into the museum.

OOOOOOOOOOOO

I wandered as fast as I could through each part of the museum to find Little Lola. I went from the Egyptian wing to the Greek and Roman wing, and then found myself in the Near Eastern **Antiquities** wing. I hated to admit it, but I was lost. I should have gotten a map before I started wandering all over the place. I knew that Little Lola was supposed to be in the Decorative Arts wing, but I couldn't find it. That is, I couldn't find it until I saw a faint green glow start to spread across the marble floors and then up the walls. Little Lola must have taken The Green Dragon out from underneath her cap!

I started to run toward the green glow repeating the phrase I'd read in Honeycutt's diary that would protect me from becoming hypnotized. All around me museum visitors fell into trances. Their eyes glazed over, some of them even sat down on the floor and just stared at the green light. I couldn't quite understand how Little Lola had gotten The Green Dragon to work. After all, she didn't know the secret words that Honeycutt had **preserved** in his diary. I didn't have time to worry about that, however. I needed to get to The Green Dragon as quickly as I could.

I ran through the paintings wing and saw both Asha Bloom and Dr. Science staring at the green glow that was **emanating** from the floor. Why weren't they stealing paintings? Their plan had completely **backfired**. They didn't take into consideration that with Little Lola in charge of The Green Dragon they were in **peril** since they too were now subject to becoming hypnotized, which from the looks of it had clearly happened. I grabbed both of them and tied them to a museum bench with my necktie. Even though they'd been victims of The Green Dragon they were still part of the plot to use it and they'd have to pay for their crimes, but they'd have to pay later—I had to get to Lola before it was too late.

As I was leaving the paintings wing I ran straight into Ian. Sadly, he had fallen victim to The Green Dragon as well. His eyes were **passive** and he just stared at the wall.

"Ian, wake up," I said, shaking him.

"I'm awake, I'm awake. Don't worry, I said the words. I'm just fascinated by this green glow. I've never seen anything like it before," Ian said.

"You mean, you're not hypnotized?" I asked.

"Nope, I feel great," he said with a smile. "And look what I found." Ian held up a giant club with sharp metal spikes **protruding** from its tip.

"Where on earth did you get that?" I asked.

"I stole it from one of the Roman weapons displays. There's no end to the usefulness of some of the stuff in this museum. Now, let's go find Aidan and your Green Dragon."

Together, we ran as fast as we could to the Decorative Arts wing, passing hypnotized visitor after hypnotized visitor. Finally, we got there. The green glow had become so bright that we had to **squint** in order to find Aidan. He tried to play the same trick on us making us think that he was hypnotized, but he wasn't.

The three of us ran to Little Lola. She was standing on a bench in the middle of a gallery. Her cap had fallen off and she was holding The Green Dragon above her head. Just as we had gotten to her Sebastian Fresh entered the gallery as well.

"That's it Little Lola, hypnotize everyone. Put everyone under your power," he shouted at her with angry **zeal**. He had something hidden underneath his arm. "Make everyone do as you wish. You're in control!" But it was very clear that Little Lola was not in control. From the look on her face you could tell that she was terrified and Sebastian wasn't helping. He was feeding her emotions which only made The Green Dragon stronger. If he kept it up, the people in the museum could end up far worse off than being hypnotized—they could end up dead.

Sparks shot from the top of The Green Dragon as Sebastian got closer and closer to Little Lola. "That's it, Lola, think about all the horrible things that have happened to you. Concentrate on how angry you feel," Sebastian said encouraging Lola to get more and more upset. Suddenly, a green flame started burning from The Green Dragon.

"I don't like this. I don't want it anymore," Lola screamed as her hands started to burn with power.

"Give it to me then," Sebastian demanded. "Give me the emerald, Lola, and it will stop." Sebastian Fresh **coveted** the power he saw **surging** through Little Lola. He would stop at nothing to get it from her.

"No," she yelled. Aidan, Ian, and I looked on in disbelief. It appeared as if Sebastian Fresh had double-crossed Dr. Science and Asha and was now trying to make poor Little Lola suffer so much that she would give up The Green Dragon to him. "You can't have it. You're evil," Lola yelled and screamed as the flame got hotter.

"Only you can stop that pain, Lola. If you give me The Green Dragon you won't feel angry anymore. You'll be happy like you used to be," Sebastian said.

"We've got to help her," Aidan said.

"I've got this club," Ian said. "What can we do?"

There was no time to **waver**. We had to come up with a plan and fast. Ian, Aidan, and I huddled and discussed a few different options and settled on the best one very **expeditiously**.

Aidan ran toward Little Lola and tackled her, knocking The Green Dragon out of her hands. Meanwhile, I went after Sebastian.

"How are you not hypnotized?" he screamed not understanding what was going on. "That's not how things are supposed to work! I'm supposed to get The Green Dragon so I can steal this painting."

The look on Sebastian's face twisted from serene to **livid** when he realized that I'd taken the painting that was hidden underneath his arm. I held it up and gazed at it. He'd stolen the most famous painting in the world, Leonardo Da Vinci's *Mona Lisa*. There she was, smiling mysteriously from inside her frame, not knowing what was happening or who'd stolen her from her place on the wall in the Louvre. Sebastian was furious.

"Give that back," he hollered and **lunged** at me losing his balance. As he fell on his face, Aidan took off his necktie and tossed it to me. I quickly wrestled Sebastian onto his stomach and tied his wrists behind his back.

The Green Dragon had fallen to the marble floor and was shooting green sparks and flames all over the gallery. Bravely, Aidan jumped on top of it and grabbed it. He stood up quickly and looked at Ian.

"Ian, would you like to play some baseball?" Aidan asked.

"You know how much I love baseball," Ian responded and held up the giant club he'd taken from the Roman weapon display.

Aidan wound up his arm and pitched The Green Dragon toward Ian. It was shooting green sparks and flames in all different directions, but Ian didn't get distracted. Ian swung the heavy club as hard as he could, keeping his eye on the emerald. When the club and The Green Dragon made contact with each other, there was a massive explosion. Hundreds of thousands of tiny little green emeralds rained down onto the gallery floor. The Green Dragon had been destroyed.

"Nice hit," Aidan said to Ian.

"Thanks, I'm a bit out of practice."

The two of them started laughing while Sebastian Fresh started to cry. "My beautiful emerald, destroyed. Do you know what you've done?" he sobbed trying to squirm free. I went over to Little Lola who had a few scrapes and bruises, but didn't appear to be seriously injured. She got up and sat back down on the bench while a few other museum guards and the museum **curator** brought Asha and Dr. Science into the gallery and put them next to Sebastian Fresh.

"You're all under arrest," the museum curator said. "Well, all of you except the guards and the little girl."

"But it wasn't us," Dr. Science said.

"It was all his fault," Asha whined, trying to kick Sebastian Fresh. "He's the one who wanted to steal the paintings. All I wanted was a pretty pair of sunglasses."

Sebastian, Dr. Science, and Asha Bloom continued to argue over whose fault it was, even up to the point they were placed into the back of the police cars. I knew without a shred of doubt that the three of them would be spending a very long time behind bars.

Little Lola picked up the *Mona Lisa* and returned it to the curator. "I'm so sorry to have caused all this trouble."

"Well, it was a bit of a mess, but without you we would have never **apprehended** those thieves. You've done a good job, Agent Lola."

Agent Lola? What on earth? Lola was a spy too? I was completely confused. All this time Lola and I had been after the same thing, to destroy The Green Dragon. Without saying a word, Lola put her cap back on her head and winked at me while Aidan and Ian began to sweep up the tiny remnants of The Green Dragon on the marble floor in the Decorative Arts gallery.

OOOOOOOOOOO

Back in my cat disguise, I left the Louvre and reviewed the past events and smiled thinking about all the criminals, kings, and all around crazy people I'd encountered: The Elephant King in the Menagerie, Sidney Whitehall, Candy Cottonshank, Jagger Powerforce, King Bruce and Veronica, and the rest of them all flashed before my eyes.

For the time being I allowed myself to feel satisfied. The Green Dragon had been destroyed and the culprits behind the whole thing had been put away. But spies are never completely satisfied with the work they do. There's always something else that's about to happen. I walked out into the streets of Paris not knowing where I'd end up next, but knew that soon enough I'd be back on the trail of some nasty fugitive.

Relationships

Decide what type of relationship the words below have to each other. If the words have similar meanings, write "S" next to the pair of words. If they have different or opposite meanings, write "O" next to the words.

1. conceal :: hide
2. covet :: desire
3. vivid :: bland
4. recur :: repeat
5. impractical :: useful
6. relinquish :: abandon
7. discriminate :: victimize
8. repulsive :: beautiful
9. crepes :: pancakes
10. disparage :: compliment
11. generic :: specific
12. relentless :: determined
13. syllable :: sound
14. evade :: avoid
15. divulge :: keep secret
16. serene :: calm
17. futile :: hopeless
18. discount :: diminish
19. stagnant :: moving
20. fidelity :: disloyalty
21. persuade :: convince

22. sympathy :: indifference
23. vanquish :: conquer
24. utter :: say

Fill in the Blank

Choose the word that best completes each of the following sentences.

1. Vanessa felt a lot of _____ toward her roommate when he didn't wash his dishes.

   a. sorrow

   b. happiness

   c. animosity

   d. humility

2. Mrs. Lawson got upset with her son for _____ all over town in her car without paying for any gas.

   a. gallivanting

   b. disappearing

   c. wavering

   d. hopping

3. The _____ victim of the accident was sadly Mrs. Fritz's cat.

    a. fluffy

    b. hapless

    c. upset

    d. hypocritical

4. Jennifer grew up to be a/an _____ for abused children.

    a. agent

    b. worker

    c. menace

    d. advocate

5. Terry couldn't help but _____ when he caught the biggest fish.

    a. lie

    b. laugh

    c. gloat

    d. appease

6. Jim always thought that being served snails was a personal _____ to his appetite.

   a. deterrent

   b. hindrance

   c. provocation

   d. affront

7. Being raised by a pack of wolves may have an influence on whether or not you're a _____.

   a. heathen

   b. canine

   c. menace

   d. brat

8. Kerry came to the meeting prepared with a specific _____ in mind.

   a. idea

   b. question

   c. generic

   d. agenda

9. Although Laura constantly contradicted herself, she still hated being called a _____.

    a. heathen

    b. hypocrite

    c. menace

    d. foolish

10. Dr. Samuels was known for his _____ lectures on good hygiene.

    a. boring

    b. fickle

    c. specific

    d. verbose

11. Chuck's father _____ his allowance when Chuck started doing more chores around the house.

    a. decreased

    b. augmented

    c. sold

    d. finished

12. Sarah felt embarrassed when she noticed that Debbie was wearing a/an _____ dress.

   a. brown

   b. frilly

   c. ripped

   d. identical

13. A.J. took too much delight in _____ his history teacher.

   a. vexing

   b. ignoring

   c. wavering

   d. imitating

14. Mark kept his room completely _____ because when it was messy it drove his mother crazy.

   a. dusted

   b. indefinite

   c. immaculate

   d. freezing

15. Gloria's opinion _____ from "yes," to "no," frequently.

    a. flip-flops

    b. wavers

    c. skips

    d. falters

16. Steven often said he was sorry just to _____ the temper of his best friend even though he didn't really mean it.

    a. appease

    b. aggravate

    c. provoke

    d. deny

17. Mr. Swan's lawyer was very upset to hear that his new evidence was _____ in court.

    a. extraordinary

    b. relinquished

    c. inadmissible

    d. false

18. Elizabeth did her homework with a lot of
_____ which is why she was a
straight A student.

   a. sleep

   b. knowledge

   c. boredom

   d. zeal

19. Nancy was very please with the wide _____
of choices she found at the bakery.

   a. objections

   b. array

   c. chaos

   d. crepes

20. Paul couldn't make plans with his friends
because his football practice schedule was
_____.

   a. indefinite

   b. shaky

   c. torn

   d. tarnished

21. Fred was in _____ of falling off a cliff.

    a. front

    b. climax

    c. peril

    d. animosity

22. The town was in complete _____ after the hurricane.

    a. destruction

    b. chaos

    c. obliteration

    d. condemnation

23. Sharon enjoyed the night she spent in her _____ hotel suite.

    a. disparaged

    b. identical

    c. filthy

    d. lavish

24. Mr. Bloom was very proud of his perfectly _____ lawn.

   a. lavish

   b. hapless

   c. manicured

   d. generic

Matching

Match each word on the left to a word with the similar meaning on the right.

1.	tarnish	a.	criticize
2.	bias	b.	goal
3.	tartan	c.	show
4.	menace	d.	intolerance
5.	climax	e.	onlooker
6.	indecipherable	f.	outrageous
7.	condemn	g.	swallowing
8.	rouge	h.	copy
9.	objective	i.	aggravate
10.	skim	j.	squeak
11.	coo	k.	turning point
12.	obliterate	l.	spectator
13.	passive	m.	unreadable
14.	depict	n.	understand
15.	outlandish	o.	blacken
16.	persevere	p.	cooperate
17.	passerby	q.	erase
18.	emulate	r.	corrupt
19.	consumption	s.	plaid
20.	exacerbate	t.	indifferent
21.	observer	u.	blush
22.	fathom	v.	be determined
23.	participate	w.	trouble maker
24.	nefarious	x.	drink
25.	libation	y.	graze

Relationships

Decide what type of relationship the words below have to each other. If the words have similar meanings, write "S" next to the pair of words. If they have different or opposite meanings, write "O" next to the words.

1. adjust :: alter
2. adieu :: hello
3. liberated :: freed
4. employment :: job
5. unscrupulous :: moral
6. unsightly :: pretty
7. unconcerned :: carefree
8. gibberish :: nonsense
9. undisclosed :: known
10. deprive :: provide
11. hosiery :: socks
12. begrudgingly :: agreeably
13. pristine :: dirty
14. subside :: enhance
15. quibble :: argue
16. huff :: temper
17. vial :: container
18. daunted :: enthusiastic
19. blazer :: jacket

20. admission :: blockage
21. apt :: capable
22. fiddle :: mess around
23. dapper :: handsome
24. smuggle :: sneak

Matching

Match each word on the left to a word with the similar meaning on the right.

1. pledge
2. antiquities
3. preserve
4. emanating
5. backfire
6. protrude
7. squint
8. surge
9. expeditiously
10. livid
11. lunge
12. curator
13. apprehend

a. glowing
b. look
c. stick out
d. rush
e. backlash
f. angry
g. promise
h. artifacts
i. thrust
j. capture
k. quickly
l. keep
m. caretaker

Now that you're on the path to becoming a master wordsmith, here's a list of books guaranteed to hold your attention and sharpen your skills. Short stories, novels, and poetry will all enhance your vocabulary while allowing you to discover new places, cultures, and time periods. There's literally a world of adventure or exploration available in your nearest library and within every book. Simply put, reading a book is just like going on a trip, minus all the packing and plane tickets!

The following list includes books recommended by teachers, librarians, and—most importantly—other young people. Check out the books in your library, and take home the ones that seem interesting to you. If you like a book, you can ask your parents, friends, teacher, or librarian to recommend others like it. But if you're not hooked after you've read a few chapters of a book, don't worry about it. Try something else. Nobody's grading you!

Adams, Douglas. *The Hitchhiker's Guide to the Galaxy.* (Science Fiction, Humor)

The first book in a series that includes *The Restaurant at the End of the Universe; Life, the Universe, and Everything; So Long, and Thanks for All the Fish;* and *Mostly Harmless.*

Alcott, Louisa May. *Little Women.* (Classic)

Block, Francesca Lia. *Weetzie Bat.* (Contemporary Fiction)

The first book in a series which has also been published in the volume *Dangerous Angels: The Weetzie Bat Books*.

Blume, Judy. *Tiger Eyes*. (Contemporary Fiction)

Blume has written many other popular books for young people, including *Blubber* and *Just as Long as We're Together*.

Burnett, Frances Hodgson. *The Secret Garden*. (Classic)

Carroll, Lewis. *Alice's Adventures in Wonderland*. (Classic)

Alice's adventures continue in *Through the Looking Glass*.

Creech, Sharon. *Walk Two Moons*. (Contemporary Fiction)

Creech has written other novels for young people, including *Chasing Redbird* and *The Wanderer*.

Cooper, Susan. *The Dark is Rising*. (Fantasy)

The first book in the series that includes *Greenwitch, The Grey King,* and *Silver on the Tree. Over Sea, Under Stone* is the prequel to this series.

Cormier, Robert. *The Chocolate War*. (Contemporary Fiction)

Dahl, Roald. *The Witches*. (Contemporary Fiction)

Dahl has written many other acclaimed books such as *Charlie and the Chocolate Factory, The BFG, Matilda,* and *James and the Giant Peach*.

Dickinson, Emily. *The Complete Poems of Emily Dickinson.* (Poetry)

Dorris, Michael. *The Window.* (Contemporary Fiction)

Dorris also wrote about the main character of this novel, Rayona, in his debut novel, *Yellow Raft in Blue Water.*

Hinton, S. E. *The Outsiders.* (Contemporary Fiction)

S. E. Hinton wrote this novel when she was a high school junior.

Fitzgerald, John. *The Great Brain.* (Historical Fiction)

The first book in a series that includes *More Adventures of the Great Brain, Me and My Little Brain, The Great Brain at the Academy, The Great Brain Reforms, The Return of the Great Brain,* and *The Great Brain Does it Again.*

Frank, Anne. *The Diary of Anne Frank.* (Classic Nonfiction)

Frost, Robert. *The Poetry of Robert Frost.* (Poetry)

George, Jean Craighead. *Julie of the Wolves.* (Contemporary Fiction)

George has written two other books about Julie, *Julie* and *Julie's Wolf Pack,* as well as *My Side of the Mountain.*

Hughes, Langston. *The Dream Keeper and Other Poems.* (Poetry)

Konigsburg, E. L. *From the Mixed-Up Files of Mrs. Basil E. Frankweiler.* (Contemporary Fiction)

Lee, Gus. *China Boy.* (Contemporary Fiction)

Also read the sequel, *Honor and Duty.*

Lee, Harper. *To Kill a Mockingbird.* (Classic)

LeGuin, Ursula. *The Wizard of Earthsea.* (Fantasy)

The first book in a series that includes *The Tombs of Atuan, The Farthest Shore,* and *Tehanu.*

L'Engle, Madeleine. *A Wrinkle in Time.* (Science Fiction, Contemporary Fiction)

L'Engle's series about the Murry family continues in *A Swiftly Tilting Planet, A Wind in the Door,* and *Many Waters.* Also try *A Ring of Endless Light,* a favorite in her series about Vicky Austin and her family.

Lewis, C. S. *The Lion, the Witch, and the Wardrobe.* (Classic, Fantasy)

This is the first book of the seven-book series, *The Chronicles of Narnia.*

Montgomery, L. M. *Anne of Green Gables.* (Classic)

Anne Shirley's story continues in *Anne of Avonlea* and *Anne of the Island. Rainbow Valley* and *Rilla of Ingleside* are about her children. Also try Montgomery's series about Emily Starr: *Emily of New Moon, Emily Climbs,* and *Emily's Quest.*

Myers, Walter Dean. *Hoops.* (Contemporary Fiction)

Myers has written dozens of books, including *Fallen Angels* and *Monster.*

Nye, Naomi Shihab. *Habibi.* (Contemporary Fiction)

Paterson, Katherine. *Bridge to Terabithia.* (Contemporary Fiction)

Other popular books by Paterson include *The Great Gilly Hopkins, The Master Puppeteer,* and *Jacob Have I Loved.*

Paulsen, Gary. *Nightjohn.* (Historical Fiction)

Paulsen has also written a sequel, *Sarny,* as well as many adventure books, including *Hatchet,* the first in a series.

Poe, Edgar Allan. *Complete Stories and Poems of Edgar Allan Poe.* (Poetry & Fiction)

Rawls, Wilson. *Where the Red Fern Grows.* (Classic)

Rowling, J. K. *Harry Potter and the Sorcerer's Stone.* (Fantasy)

This is the first book in a wildly popular seven-book series.

Salinger, J. D. *Catcher in the Rye.* (Classic)

de Saint-Exupery, Antoine. *The Little Prince.* (Classic, Fantasy)

Soto, Gary. *Baseball in April and Other Stories.* (Contemporary Fiction)

Also try Soto's novel *Crazy Weekend,* and *Neighborhood Odes,* a collection of his poetry.

Staples, Suzanne Fisher. *Shabanu: Daughter of the Wind.* (Contemporary Fiction)

Shabanu's story continues in *Haveli.*

Taylor, Mildred D. *Roll of Thunder, Hear My Cry.* (Historical Fiction)

Tolkien, J. R. R. *The Hobbit.* (Fantasy)

The prequel to the *Lord of the Rings* series, which includes *The Fellowship of the Ring, The Two Towers,* and *The Return of the King.*

Twain, Mark. *Adventures of Huckleberry Finn.* (Classic)

This book followed *The Adventures of Tom Sawyer.*

Voigt, Cynthia. *Homecoming.* (Contemporary Fiction)

The first book about Dicey Tillerman's family and friends; others include *Dicey's Song, A Solitary Blue,* and *Seventeen Against the Dealer.*

Williams, William Carlos. *Selected Poems.* (Poetry)

Wojciechowska, Maia. *Shadow of a Bull.* (Fiction)

Yep, Laurence. *Dragonwings.* (Historical Fiction)

Also try Yep's other novels about Chinese-American life, *Child of the Owl* and *Dragon's Gate.*

Zindel, Paul. *The Pigman.* (Contemporary Fiction)

GLOSSARY

A

ABANDONED (uh-ban-duhnd) *adj.* left behind and forgotten

The children spent an exciting night in an *abandoned* barn that was supposedly haunted.

ABODE (uh-bohd) *n.* a place where someone lives; home

Meredith invited her friends into her *abode*.

ABRUPT (uh-bruhpt) *adj.* sudden or unexpected change

Anna's mood swings were *abrupt* and sometimes scary.

ABSTRACT (ab-strakt) *adj.* difficult to understand because it doesn't apply to concrete reality

Philosophy can sometimes be very *abstract*.

ACCESSORY (ak-ses-uh-ree) *n.* an article or set of articles of dress, such as gloves or earrings that adds completeness, convenience, and attractiveness to one's basic outfit

Susan added a purple, beaded necklace to her dress as an *accessory*.

ACCOMPLICE (uh-kom-plis) *n.* a person who knowingly helps another to commit a crime or wrongdoing

The *accomplice* driving the getaway car was put in jail.

ACCOMMODATION (uh-kom-uh-dey-shuhn) *n.* something that satisfies a need or desire

It was difficult to find sleeping *accommodations* in the small town.

ACUTE (uh-kyoot) *adj.* sharp and brief

The headache gave Robert an *acute* pain behind his eyes.

AD-LIB (ad-lib) *v.* to act or speak without preparation

When he forgot his lines in the school play Larry had to *ad-lib* the rest of his performance.

ADAPT (uh-dapt) *v.* to adjust oneself to different conditions or environment

Kelly decided that instead of throwing a temper tantrum it would be better to *adapt* to the situation.

ADIEU (uh-dyoo) *n.* goodbye in French

Mel said *adieu* to his guests and went to bed.

ADJACENT (uh-jey-cent) *adj.* lying near or next to

The hose was *adjacent* to the flower garden.

ADJUST (uh-juhst) *v.* to change something to make it work or fit better

Marcy *adjusted* her belt so that it fit a little more tightly around her waist.

ADMISSION (ad-mish-uhn) *n.* permission to enter

It's very hard to gain *admission* to certain historical places.

ADORN (uh-dawrn) *v.* to decorate or make pretty

Mrs. Washington *adorned* her Christmas tree with ornaments.

ADVERSE (ad-vurs) *adj.* unfavorable; difficult

Tina was faced with an *adverse* situation.

ADVOCATE (ad-vuh-kit) *n.* a person who speaks or writes in defense of another

Fritz was an *advocate* for human rights.

AFLAME (uh-fleym) *adj.* on fire

The curtains were set *aflame* by a misplaced candle.

AFFRONT (uh-fruhnt) *n.* an offense or insult

Jim felt *affronted* when his ex-girlfriend ignored him at the restaurant.

AGENDA (uh-jen-duh) *n.* a list or plan for what needs to be done

Martin feels absolutely lost if he doesn't have a daily *agenda*.

AGHAST (uh-gast) *adj.* struck with overwhelming shock or amazement

Phillip was *aghast* when he saw his grandmother on a motorcycle.

AGITATE (aj-i-teyt) *v.* to force into violent or irregular action

The sea was *agitated* by the forceful wind.

AJAR (uh-jahr) *adj.* partly open

Lola left her door slightly *ajar*.

ALIAS (ey-lee-us) *n.* a false or fake name

Rita used an *alias* whenever she published a book.

Many spies have to use an *alias*.

ALIKE (uh-lahyk) *adj.* similar or showing no important difference between

The twins were so *alike* that it was hard to tell them apart.

ALLAY (uh-ley) *v.* to lessen or calm

The cup of tea helped *allay* Ally's fears.

ALLEVIATE (uh-lee-vee-yet) *v.* to make easier

Ariel tried to *alleviate* the pain in her ankle by resting her leg on a pillow.

ALLUDE (uh-lood) *v.* to make reference to

The film title "Back to the Future" *alludes* to time-travel.

ALLURE (uh-loor) *n.* the power to entice and attract

Heather's *allure* was undeniable to anyone who attended the dance.

AMBASSADOR (am-bas-uh-der) *n.* a diplomatic official sent by one country to another country as its representative

Vince was moved by the *ambassador's* speech about peace.

AMOROUS (am-er-uhs) *adj.* involving love

Patty was excited to receive an *amorous* letter from her boyfriend.

ANCESTORS (an-ses-ters) *n.* pl. people from whom one is descended

Margot was claiming that George Washington was one of her *ancestors*.

Our country's *ancestors* endured many hardships.

ANECDOTE (an-ik-doht) *n.* a humorous short tale or story

Tony told his teacher an *anecdote* about how his homework had strangely disappeared.

Miriam laughed at her mother's *anecdote* about the mailman.

ANIMOSITY (an-uh-mos-i-tee) *n.* a feeling of ill will or dislike

Natasha had a certain amount of *animosity* toward her sister's boyfriend.

ANTICIPATE (an-tis-uh-peyt) *v.* to look forward to

Jen was *anticipating* the arrival of her new books in the mail.

ANTIQUITIES (an-tik-wi-tees) *n.* pl. things from the past; relics

Silvia's grandfather has a large collection of war *antiquities*.

ANTONYM (an-tuh-nim) *n.* a word having the opposite meaning of another word

Sad is an *antonym* for happy.

ANXIETY (ang-zhay-i-tee) *n.* uneasiness or nervousness in the mind caused by the fear that something bad might happen

Suzanne could not control her *anxiety* the day before school started.

APATHY (ap-uh-thee) *n.* lack of interest or concern; passionless

Steve's *apathy* about making his bed was more than obvious.

APPEASE (uh-peez) *v.* to pacify, calm, or soothe

Jerry was sick of trying to *appease* his cranky mother.

APPREHEND (ap-ri-hend) *v.* to take into legal custody; to stop or arrest

Rita yelled for the police to *apprehend* the man who had just stolen her purse.

APT (apt) *adj.* well-suited to the given purpose

John was *apt* at playing the piano because he practiced whenever he could.

AROUSE (uh-rouz) *v.* to provoke to action or response

When he heard his dog bark Freddy's suspicions were *aroused*.

ARRAY (uh-rey) *n.* a large grouping of things; variety

There was a wide *array* of things to do at the carnival.

ARTICULATE (ahr-tik-yuh-lit) *adj.* having the ability to use words well

Jack's English teacher was very impressed with how *articulate* he was.

ASCERTAIN (as-er-teyn) *v.* to find out definitively

Tim wanted to *ascertain* whether or not school had been cancelled due to the snow storm.

ASSERT (uh-sert) *v.* to state with confidence

Halle *asserts* her opinions in class often.

ASSOCIATE (uh-soh-shee-eyt) *n.* a person who is united with another person; a colleague or business partner

Matthew and Jennifer were *associates* through the tennis association in their neighborhood.

ASSUAGE (uh-swej) *v.* to make less severe

Byron *assuaged* his grandmother's fears about going to the dentist.

ASSURE (uh-shur) *v.* to pledge or state with confidence

Felix *assured* his boss that the business reports would be finished by Monday.

ASTUTE (uh-stoot) *adj.* clever or cunning

Diane had an *astute* plan to get a ticket to the movie even though it was sold out.

ATROCIOUS (uh-troh-shuhs) *adj.* extremely bad or shockingly dreadful

The monkey's table manners were absolutely *atrocious*.

AVAIL (uh-veyl) *n.* advantage or effective use of an object or goal

Amy looked for a job to no *avail*.

AVERSION (uh-ver-zhuhn) *n.* a strong feeling of dislike

Bonnie had an *aversion* to seafood.

AUGMENT (awg-ment) *v.* to make larger

Harold's salary was *augmented* by a number of bonuses.

AUSTERE (aw-steer) *adj.* somber or serious in appearance

Many people think that cemeteries are *austere* places.

AWKWARD (awk-werd) *adj.* lack of social or physical grace

James was known to be both clumsy and *awkward*.

Nicole felt very *awkward* when her teacher asked about her best friend cheating on the test.

B

BACKFIRE (bak-fahyr) *v.* to bring an opposite result from that which was planned or expected

Cindy's plan to have a birthday party while her parents were out of town totally *backfired* because they returned home early.

BAFFLE (baf-uhl) *v.* to confuse

Tamara liked to *baffle* her dog by pretending to throw a ball when she actually didn't even have one.

BANE (beyn) *n.* something or someone that ruins or spoils

Doing the dishes was the *bane* of Rebecca's existence.

BANAL (buh-nal) *adj.* boring or unoriginal

Steven found himself yawning during his manager's *banal* speech about customer service.

Trudie found that her days at the office grew more and more *banal*.

BARRAGE (buh-rahzh) *n.* a large quantity or explosion of words, insults, or blows

Berlin suffered a *barrage* of bombings during World War II.

The president was asked a *barrage* of questions by the reporters.

BASE (beys) *adj.* not refined; morally low

Dina was embarrassed by her son using such *base* language.

BECKON (bek-uhn) *v.* to signal by nodding or waving someone over to join you

Maria *beckoned* to the waiter for him to bring her the check.

BEGRUDGE (bi-gruhj) *v.* to resent or be jealous

Pete *begrudged* the fact that Jason was so talented at sports.

BEHOLDEN (bi-hohl-duhn) *adj.* obligated

Katie was *beholden* to no one.

BEHOOVE (bi-hoov) *v.* to be necessary or proper

The situation *behooves* an apology.

BELLIGERENT (buh-lij-er-uhnt) *adj.* eager to start a fight

Frank was feeling *belligerent* during detention which is why he was expelled.

BENEFICIAL (ben-uh-fish-uhl) *adj.* helpful and advantageous

The new medication had a *beneficial* effect on the patient.

BENEVOLENT (buh-nev-uh-luhnt) *adj.* characterized by a desire to spread goodwill or help others

The donation was made by a *benevolent* gentleman.

BENIGN (bi-nahyn) *adj.* having a kindly or gentle disposition

Gertrude has a *benign* smile.

BIAS (bahy-uhs) *n.* an inclination to think a certain way or to hold something in higher favor than something else

Jenny had a *bias* for silk, which she preferred even to velvet.

BINGE (binj) *v.* excessive eating or drinking

Amy loved to *binge* on licorice at slumber parties.

BLACKMAIL (blak-meyl) *v.* to force someone to do something by threatening them

Oliver claimed that he was *blackmailed* into giving his confession.

BLAND (bland) *adj.* lacking in flavor

Cassie's mom makes very *bland* chili.

BLATANT (bleyt-nt) *adj.* completely obvious

Stacey told her parents a *blatant* lie about why she was late for dinner.

BLAZER (bley-zer) *n.* a sports jacket

Mr. Williams couldn't sit down in the restaurant without wearing a tie and *blazer.*

BLEAK (bleek) *adj.* without hope

Although there was snow on the ground, the small amount made the outcome of school being cancelled look rather *bleak.*

BODE (bahyd) *v.* to predict or tell beforehand

The news did not *bode* well for Johnny.

BOISTEROUS (boi-ster-uhs) *adj.* noisy and rowdy

The sound of the students' laughter was quite *boisterous.*

BOHEMIAN (bo-hee-mee-uhn) *adj.* unconventional and free of rules

Rob decided that a *bohemian* lifestyle suited him best, so he joined an artist's colony and started to paint.

BOVINE (boh-vahyn) *adj.* cow-like

Shelly's Halloween costume made her appear particularly *bovine.*

BLUNDER (bluhn-der) *n.* a gross, stupid, or careless mistake

Frank finally realized what a *blunder* it had been to yell at his best friend for no reason.

BRAINSTORM (breyen-stawrm) *v.* to think of many different solutions or ideas, sometimes in a large group

The housing committee tried to *brainstorm* a better way to handle offensive lawn ornaments in their neighborhood.

BRAWN (brawn) *n.* muscular strength

Jake had a surprising amount of *brawn* despite his small size.

BREACH (breech) *n.* a break or rupture in a system

There was a *breach* in the water pipe that caused the basement to flood.

BROACH (brohch) *v.* to mention or bring up a subject

Natalie *broached* the topic of going on a skiing trip with her parents.

BRISKLY (brisk-lee) *adv.* quick and lively

We *briskly* walked to the lake.

BUREAUCRACY (byoo-rok-ruh-see) *n.* the administrative structure of a large or complex organization

The company's *bureaucracy* dictates that all paper used must be yellow.

C

CAHOOTS (kah-hoots) *n. pl.* to be in partnership

Alex and Annie were in *cahoots* with each other.

CALIBER (kal-uh-ber) *n.* degree of quality

Russia is known for producing caviar of the highest *caliber.*

CALLOUS (kal-uhs) *adj.* insensitive or unsympathetic

Years and years of disappointment would make anyone a bit *callous.*

CAMARADERIE (kam-er-ahd-er-ee) *n.* spirit of friendship or good humor

Despite their differences, the three musketeers shared a strong sense of *camaraderie.*

CAMOUFLAGE (kam-uh-flahzh) *v.* to hide or disguise or *n.* a disguise.

To *camouflage* the pimple she had, Anne used a lot of make-up on her chin.

The *camouflage* hid the soldiers from their enemies.

CANDID (kan-did) *adj.* honest and outspoken.

The doctor was very *candid* about his patients' medical conditions.

CANINE (key-nahyn) *adj.* dog-like or *n.* dog

Aunt Carol often complained of being woken up by *canine* noises in the middle of the night.

Being a *canine*, Lassie knew well how to bark.

CANNIBAL (kan-i-buhl) *n.* a person who eats human flesh

The *cannibals* in the movie were portrayed in a negative way.

CAPACITY (kuh-pas-i-tee) *n.* the maximum amount that can be contained

The concert was sold-out and the theater was at its full *capacity*.

CAPTIVATED (kap-tuh-veyt-ed) *adj.* to have one's attention held fully by something or someone

Mr. Hullings was *captivated* by his favorite television show.

CARICATURE (kar-i-kuh-cher) *n.* a representation of something that exaggerates its subjects' features or characteristics

The *caricature* of the politician on the morning newspaper's comics page was hilarious.

CASUALTY (kazh-oo-uhl-tee) *n.* one who is injured or killed in an accident

Candace's brother was a *casualty* of war.

CENSOR (sen-ser) *v.* to prevent any material, such as books or movies, that are considered offensive or harmful from being seen

It should be wrong to *censor* anyone's speech.

CHAFE (cheyf) *v.* to make sore by rubbing together

During the marathon, Martin's thighs began to *chafe*.

CHAOS (kay-os) *n.* a state of total disorder and confusion

Winston's room was frequently so messy that his friends said it was in a constant state of *chaos*.

CHARADE (shuh-reyd) *n.* an obvious deception

Victor didn't want to sit through the *charade* of the politician's apology.

CHIC (sheek) *adj.* style and elegance especially in dress

Cate was known for her *chic* appearance.

CHISEL (chiz-uhl) *n.* a wedge-like tool used for cutting and shaping wood or stone

The artist used a *chisel* to sculpt his statue.

CIVILIAN (si-vil-yuhn) *n.* a nonmilitary citizen

Mrs. Smith was disgusted with the number of *civilian* deaths that were reported on the evening news.

CLARIFY (klar-i-fahy) *v.* to make clear or understandable

Molly asked her teacher to *clarify* the assignment.

CLAMOR (kalm-er) *n.* a loud, continuous noise

The *clamor* from the road construction was driving Daisy insane.

The cat made a *clamor* when it knocked the dish off the counter.

CLERGY (klur-jee) *n.* a group of people ordained for religious service

The *clergy* was known for their charitable acts.

CLICHÉ (klee-shey) *adj.* an expression or thought that has lost its originality because it has been used too many times

Some think that modern art has become nothing but *cliché*.

Every word that comes out of Carol's mouth is so *clichéd*.

CLIMAX (klahy-maks) the highest and most intense point of development

The *climax* of the novel was so exciting that Boris couldn't put the book dow*n*.

COINCIDE (koh-in-seyd) *v.* to happen at the same time or to occupy the same space

Our neighbor's vacation time *coincided* with ours.

COMMEND (kuh-mend) *v.* to praise as worthy

The senator *commended* the cadet on his performance.

COMPILE (kuh-m-pahyl) *v.* to put together

The Yellow Pages *compiles* all the phone numbers for the companies located in the city.

COMPLACENT (kuhm-pley-suhnt) *adj.* pleased about something

The athlete was *complacent* with his fantastic performance on the field.

COMPLY (kuhm-plahy) *v.* to act within someone's wishes or requests

The garbage man had to *comply* with his partner's wishes to turn the radio's volume down.

COMPONENT (kom-poh-nuhnt) *n.* an important part, element or ingredient

The brakes were the missing *component* to Mr. Davidson's car.

COMPREHEND (kom-pre-hend) *v.* to understand the meaning or nature of something

Eve couldn't *comprehend* why her dog kept getting sick.

COMPROMISING (kom-pruh-mayhz-ing) *adj.* to be exposed to danger or embarrassment

Being alone in the woods is a *compromising* position.

CONCEAL (kuhn-seel) *v.* to keep something from being seen

Cindy tried to *conceal* her real identity because she was working under cover.

CONCILIATORY (kuhn-cil-ee-uh-tawr-ee) *adj.* willing to compromise

Susan was *conciliatory* once she heard the terms of the deal.

Dr. Golding was not *conciliatory* when it came to the well-being of his patients.

CONCLUDE (kuh-n-klood) *v.* to come to a final decision

Patty *concluded* that her headache was caused by stress.

CONCOCTION (kon-kok-shuhn) *n.* a strange or unusual mixture

Brian was surprised when the *concoction* he'd mixed in his chemistry lab turned bright green.

CONDEMN (kuhn-dem) *v.* to express an unfavorable judgment upon

The old house was *condemned* because of its poor rundown condition.

CONDENSE (kohn-dens) *v.* to make more compact; to combine

Mandy decided to *condense* the contents of her shirt drawer and her pants drawer.

CONDONE (kuhn-dohn) *v.* to overlook or disregard something objectionable or illegal

Judge Franklin could not *condone* the criminal's past behavior.

CONSPICUOUS (kuhn-spik-yoo-uhs) *adj.* easily seen or noticeable

Diana thought her new haircut made her look far too *conspicuous*.

CONSPIRACY (kuhn-spir-uh-see) *n.* an unlawful, secret, or evil plan or purpose

Kelly devised a *conspiracy* to destroy the student government.

CONSUMPTION (kuhn-suhmp-shuhn) *n.* the amount used

The United States of America has a high *consumption* of gasoline.

CONTRADICT (kon-truh-dikt) *v.* to speak or act against or to say or do the opposite

Mr. Black's feelings *contradicted* what he was saying.

CONTRARY (kon-trer-ee) *adj.* opposite in nature or character

Contrary to Jack's opinion, Jamie was driving too fast.

Samantha's idea of what was a healthy snack was *contrary* to that of her mother's.

CONTEMPLATE (kon-tuhm-pleyt) *v.* to think deeply or seriously

Edward *contemplated* the nature of death.

CONTEMPT (kuh-n-tempt) *n.* the feeling of regarding someone or something as inferior or worthless

Mr. Phillips viewed his co-workers with a lot of *contempt* because he thought he was better at his job than they were.

CONTENT (kuhn-tent) *adj.* satisfied with what you have

Lisa was *content* with the B+ she received on her research paper.

CONVALESCE (kon-vuh-les) *v.* to recuperate or re-cover

Nan helped her grandmother *convalesce* after surgery.

COO (koo) *v.* to murmur soft sounds similar to the noise a dove makes

The baby *cooed* in its cradle.

CORPSE (kawrps) a dead body

Julia's neighbors put a fake *corpse* on their porch for Halloween.

COVET (kuh-vit) *v.* to wrongfully desire

May *covets* her sister's car.

CRÊPE (kreyp) *n.* a thin, light pancake

The children enjoyed a breakfast of strawberry-covered *crêpes*.

CRISIS (krahy-sis) *n.* an unstable situation; a dangerous situation

The city was in *crisis* after the earthquake.

CULINARY (kyoo-luh-ner-ee) *adj.* pertaining to cooking

Justin decided to drop out of college and attend *culinary* school instead.

CULPRIT (kuhl-prit) *n.* a person guilty of a fault or a crime

Greg was the *culprit* behind the broken vase.

CULT (kuhlt) *n.* members of a group who participate in specific and secretive ceremonies

Mindy thought it might be a good idea to join a gym and become part of the physical fitness *cult*.

Daniel ran away from home and joined a strange religious *cult*.

CUMBERSOME (kuhm-ber-suhm) *adj.* characterized by being a burden; troublesome

Letting relatives stay with you is more often than not very *cumbersome*.

CURATOR (kyoor-ey-tor) *n.* the person in charge of an art collection or museum

The *curator* was furious when he found out that a collection of priceless vases had been broken.

CURSORY (kur-suh-ree) *adj.* rapidly going over something without paying attention to the details

Brandon gave a *cursory* look at his homework before he went out with his friends.

CURT (kurt) *adj.* rude and short in speech or manner

Mr. Billings was very upset about his daughter's *curt* telephone call.

CYNIC (sin-ik) *n.* a person who believes that most people are only motivated by selfishness

Ronald accused Diane of being a *cynic*.

D

DABBLE (dab-uhl) *v.* to do something without serious intent

Mr. Hughes *dabbled* in painting as a hobby.

DAPPER (dap-er) *adj.* neat and tidy; clean cut

Sidney looked very *dapper* in his new suit.

DAUNTED (dawnt-ed) *adj.* to be discouraged

Annie felt *daunted* by the amount of books she had to carry home from the library.

DEBAUCHERY (di-baw-chuh-ree) *n.* overindulgence in pleasures usually considered immoral

Jesse's life of *debauchery* eventually landed him in prison.

DEBACLE (dey-bah-kuhl) *n.* a complete failure

Mrs. Easton's tea party was a *debacle*.

DEBRIS (duh-bree) *n.* the remains of anything broken down

After the hurricane the city was full of *debris*.

DECAPITATE (di-kap-i-teyt) *v.* to behead

Miranda was furious when she found out that her little brother had *decapitated* her favorite.

DECLAIM (di-kleym) *v.* to say something in a pompous manner

Donald *declaimed* that he'd like to be the president of a rich company someday.

DECOY (dee-koi) *n.* something used to lure someone into a trap

The duck hunters set up a *decoy* to lure their prey.

DEEM (deem) *v.* to form an opinion

The coach did not *deem* it necessary for his players to warm up before the game.

DEFECT (dee-fekt) *n.* an imperfection or fault

Tony bought the sweater with the *defect* because it was less expensive.

DEGRADE (dee-greyd) *v.* to lower in value or opinion; to insult

Megan *degrades* herself in front of other people too much.

DEJECTION (di-jek-shuhn) *n.* lowness of spirit; depression

Claire felt a sense of *dejection* when she wasn't chosen to be on the cheerleading squad.

DELIBERATELY (di-lib-er-ehyt-lee) ad*v.* intentional; something done on purpose

Fred *deliberately* ignored his teacher and didn't do his science homework.

Judy crossed the street *deliberately* to avoid her neighbor's dog.

DELIRIOUS (di-leer-ee-uhs) *adj.* characterized by uncontrolled excitement

Zoe was *delirious* with joy after hearing the good news.

DENOUNCE (di-nouns) *v.* to condemn openly as being evil or reprehensible

James *denounced* his dog as the criminal who ate his homework.

The criminal was *denounced* in a court of law.

DENSE (dens) *adj.* closely compacted together; crowded

Mandy tried to move through the *dense* crowd quickly so as to keep up with her tour guide.

DEPICT (di-pikt) *v.* to portray or represent

The painting *depicted* a lovely picnic.

DEPLETE (di-pleet) to seriously decrease the amount or supply of something

The rainforests have been *depleted* by land developers.

DEPRIVE (di-prahyv) *v.* to withhold something from being enjoyed

Morgan *deprived* herself of ice cream for a whole week while she was on a diet.

DERIDE (di-rahyd) *v.* to scorn or laugh at

Mr. Fulton *derided* his students for trying to pull a prank on him.

DESCENT (di-sent) *n.* moving lower

The children started their *descent* into the hidden cave at midnight.

DESPITE (di-spahyt) *prep.* in spite of

Amanda laughed off the argument *despite* the fact that she was actually upset.

DETER (di-tur) *v.* to discourage or try to prevent

The barking dogs *deterred* robbers from breaking into the house.

Sadie used a car alarm to *deter* theft.

DEVOUR (di-vour) *v.* to consume or swallow up

Mike *devoured* his ham and cheese sandwich.

DIDACTIC (dahy-dak-tik) *adj.* instructive or intended to teach something

Brad got bored during the principal's *didactic* lecture on good behavior.

DIGNITARY (dig-ni-ter-ee) *n.* a person who holds a high rank or office, such as in the government or a church

Mr. Goldworthy was a visiting *dignitary* from France.

DIGNITY (dig-ni-tee) *n.* elevation of character or worthiness

Wearing his father's military medal gave Jackson a great sense of *dignity*.

DILEMMA (di-lem-uh) *n.* a difficult situation or problem

Frank found himself with a *dilemma* on his hands when he'd found out that his bike had been stolen.

DILIGENT (dil-i-juh-nt) *adj.* attentive and persistent; a constant effort

Mary is *diligent* about keeping her room clean.

DISCIPLINE (dis-uh-plin) *n.* a branch of instruction or study

Eric chose to study art as his *discipline*.

DISCLOSE (di-sklohz) *v.* to make known or out in the open

Dr. Jennings could not *disclose* the cause of his patient's headache.

DISCORD (dis-kawrd) *n.* difference in opinion; a disagreement

There was a certain amount of *discord* between the two chess players about what was the best way to start a chess game.

DISCOUNT (dis-kount) *v.* to subtract value from something

The van was *discounted* because it was used.

Mary *discounted* the fact that her sister was very good at gymnastics.

DISCREET (di-skreet) *adj.* able to show self-restraint with regard to keeping something secret

Joseph told his Aunt Mildred everything because she promised to be *discreet.*

DISCRIMINATE (di-skrim-uh-neyt) *v.* to show prejudice or make distinctions on the base of class, race, or appearance rather than personal merit

Holly felt *discriminated* against because of her religious beliefs.

DISDAIN (dis-deyn) *n.* a feeling of contempt for anything thought of as unworthy

Michael had a great amount of *disdain* for his friend's taste in music.

DISMAYED (dis-mae-d) *v.* to be upset or alarmed

Trina was *dismayed* that she missed her bus.

DISORIENTED (dis-awr-ee-ent-ed) *adj.* out of touch; confused about place or time

Mitch always felt *disoriented* when he woke up.

DISPARAGE (di-spar-ij) *v.* to belittle or speak slightingly

Martha was upset with her cousin for *disparaging* their grandfather's generosity.

DISPASSIONATE (dis-pash-uh-nit) *adj.* unaffected by emotion or personal feeling

The police officer tried to remain *dispassionate* while he arrested the group of protestors.

DISSENT (di-sent) *n.* difference of sentiment or opinion

There was some *dissent* among the crowd about who was first in line.

DISTRACT (di-strakt) *v.* to divert attention from

Austin was *distracted* by the fireworks.

DIVERSE (di-vurs) *adj.* various forms or kinds

The crowd was full of *diverse* people.

DIVULGE (di-vuhlj) *v.* to reveal or make known

The press *divulged* the story about the newly born panda bear.

It takes a lot of discipline not to *divulge* a secret.

DOGMATIC (dawg-mat-ik) *adj.* characterized by arrogant opinions of something that cannot be proven

Many politicians have *dogmatic* beliefs.

DOMAIN (doh-meyn) *n.* an area under control of a ruler

Jake's dog thought that the back yard was his *domain.*

DON (dohn) *v.* to put on clothing

Sara *donned* her soccer uniform before the big game.

DORMITORY (dawr-mi-taw-ree) *n.* a room containing several beds

The students returned to their *dormitory* to sleep after dinner.

DOTE (doht) *v.* to habitually express love or fondness

Mark *dotes* on his puppy.

DOWNTRODDEN (doun-trod-n) oppressed or held back

Walter felt *downtrodden* after he'd been fired from his job.

DUB (duhb) *v.* to name or give a title

Luke was very proud the day that the queen *dubbed* him a knight.

Jill happily *dubbed* her dog Fluffy.

DUBIOUS (doo-bee-uhs) *adj.* doubtful or uncertain

Lyn felt *dubious* about her college entrance exams.

DUPED (doop-ed) *v.* to be fooled or tricked

Mark was *duped* to believe that his blind date was intelligent when, in fact, she was not.

DUPLICATED (doo-pli-keyt-ed) *v.* replicated or copied exactly like the original

The sculptures in Mrs. Jackson's yard were obviously *duplicated*.

DURABLE (door-uh-buhl) *adj.* lasting; enduring

Mel was glad that he had a *durable* lunchbox instead of a paper sack.

DURATION (doo-rey-shuhn) *n.* the length or period of time that something lasts

Bill was told to keep quiet for the *duration* of the meeting.

DUSK (duhsk) *n.* partial darkness between daytime and nighttime; sunset

As *dusk* approached, the campers put up their tents and gathered wood to build a fire.

E

EARMARK (eer-mahrk) *v.* to set aside or mark for a specific purpose

Steve *earmarked* the page in his book so he'd remember which page he should start reading again.

EARNEST (ur-nist) *adj.* serious and sincere

Judy gave her mother an *earnest* apology after she'd forgotten to fold the laundry.

EAVESDROP (eevz-drop) *v.* to secretly listen in on a private conversation

Carl put a glass against the door so that he could *eavesdrop* on his parents' conversation.

EBB (eb) *v.* to recede

Vicky watched the tide *ebb* and flow while the sun set.

ECCENTRIC (ik-sen-trik) *adj.* odd or strange

Walking your dog backwards is rather *eccentric*.

ECSTASY (ek-stuh-see) *n.* an overpowering emotional state of pleasure

Many say that being in love is complete *ecstasy*.

EGO (ee-goh) *n.* self-esteem or self-image

Julie has a huge *ego*.

ELUDE (i-lood) *v.* to avoid by cleverness.

Susan *eluded* all the questions that her mother asked about her whereabouts.

EMANATE (em-uh-neyt) *v.* to flow out

Joy was *emanating* from Harold's face.

EMBARGO (em-bahr-goh) *n.* a restriction on commerce

The oil *embargo* affected the price of gasoline.

EMBERS (em-bers) *n.* the remains of a fire

The *embers* glowed softly in the fireplace.

EMERGE (i-murj) *v.* to come up or forth

The caterpillar *emerged* from its cocoon as a butterfly

EMULATE (em-yuh-leyt) *v.* to imitate or try to copy

Doreen tried to *emulate* her older sister's behavior.

EMPLOYMENT (em-ploi-muhnt) *n.* the state of being employed or employing someone; having or offering a job

Ariel's *employment* was dependant on how well she did on the placement test.

EN ROUTE (ahn-root) adv. on the way

We were *en route* to the bank when we heard it had been robbed.

ENAMORED (in-am-erd) *adj.* delighted with or unreasonably in love with

Jane was totally *enamored* with Peter despite his lack of interest in her.

ENCRUSTED (en-krust-ed) *v.* decorated or inlayed with different materials

My grandfather's cane was *encrusted* with ivory.

Julie's ring is *encrusted* with diamonds and rubies.

ENDORSE (en-dawrs) *v.* to approve or give support

The politician's campaign was *endorsed* by several big businesses.

ENGROSS (en-grohs) *v.* to completely occupy one's attention

Beth was too *engrossed* in her work to notice that she missed lunch.

ENIGMA (uh-nig-muh) *n.* an inexplicable situation or person

The disappearance of Fred's cat was a complete *enigma*.

ENSUE (en-soo) *v.* to follow in order; to come after something

A paycheck *ensues* after a lot of hard work.

ENVY (en-vee) *n.* a feeling of jealousy in regard to someone else's advantages or success

Britney was full of *envy* when she heard that Shelly had been chosen for the school play.

ESPIONAGE (es-pee-uh-nahzh –nij) *n.* the act or practice of spying

Sam was accused of *espionage* by a foreign government.

EQUILIBRIUM (ee-kwuh-lib-ree-uhm) *n.* a state of balance

Since he broke his leg, Jeff's *equilibrium* has been slightly different.

EQUIPPED (i-kwip-d) *adj.* to be provided or supplied with the right tools for any given purpose

The playground is properly *equipped* with swings and monkey bars.

ERADICATE (i-rad-i-keyt) *v.* to completely destroy

The coach *eradicated* Cliff's hopes of joining the basketball team.

ESSENTIAL (uh-sen-shuhl) *adj.* completely necessary

Most doctors will tell you that fruits and vegetables are an *essential* part to any healthy diet.

ESTEEM (i-steem) *n.* a high regard or respect for someone or something

> Matt held his best friend in high *esteem*.
>
> Julie's self-*esteem* had been suffering.

ESTIMATE (es-tuh-meyt) *v.* to guess or form an approximate judgment

> Harry *estimated* that it would take five days for the books he ordered to arrive at his house.

ETIQUETTE (et-i-kit) *n.* rules of conduct and behavior established in any class or community or for any occasion; manners

> Laura's *etiquette* at the wedding was appalling.

EVACUATE (i-vak-yoo-yet) *v.* to leave or vacate

> The people in the city had to *evacuate* their homes due to an impending hurricane.

EVADE (i-veyd) *v.* to avoid or escape

> Alex *evaded* his uncle's questions by quickly changing the subject.

EUPHONY (yoo-fuh-nee) *n.* pleasing effect to the ear; harmonious

> The choir produced a majestic *euphony* for its audience.

EXACERBATE (ig-zas-er-beyt) *v.* to irritate or annoy

> The chalk scratching on the chalkboard only seemed to *exacerbate* the students' irritation.

EXASPERATING (ik-zas-puh-reyt-ing) *adj.* extremely annoying

> Nicole's temper tantrums were *exasperating*.

EXCAVATE (eks-kuh-veyt) *v.* to dig or scoop out

> Juliet spent the summer *excavating* dinosaur fossils in North Dakota.

EXCEPTION (ik-sep-shuhn) *n.* an instance or case that doesn't conform to the general rule

Marcus made an *exception* to his rule of never being late because he wanted to see the end of the movie.

EXHAUST (ig-zawst) *v.* to drain of strength; to completely use up

The marathon *exhausted* most of the runners.

EXODUS (ek-suh-duhs) *n.* a departure of a large number of people

Bill and his family joined the *exodus* of people going to the beach to enjoy the beautiful weather.

EXPEDIENT (ik-spee-dee-uhnt) *adj.* suitable for the purpose at hand

It was *expedient* for Marcy to leave the party early.

EXPEDITE (ek-spi-dahyt) *v.* to speed up the process of something

Ani was going to have to *expedite* the shipping of her passport from home if she wanted to travel out of the country.

EXPEDITION (ek-spi-dish-uhn) *n.* a journey or voyage made for a specific purpose

Dave went on an *expedition* to find the perfect piece of pie.

EXPEDITIOUS (ek-spi-dish-uhs) *adj.* characterized by quickness; prompt

Lucy's response to her friend's e-mail was *expeditious*.

EXPLICIT (ik-splis-it) *adj.* described or shown in realistic detail

The plan to rob the ice cream store was mapped out, making it perfectly *explicit*.

EXPLOIT (ik-sploit) *v.* to selfishly use something or someone for one's own personal gain

Lacey *exploited* her sister's generosity by overstaying her welcome.

EXPONENTIAL (ek-spoh-nen-shuhl) *adj.* increasing or decreasing numerically

Ted feared that the value his collection of baseball cards was decreasing at an *exponential* rate.

EXTRACT (ik-strakt) *v.* to pull out

The dentist *extracted* five of Donna's teeth.

EXTRAORDINARY (ik-strawr-dn-er-ee) *adj.* beyond what is usual or ordinary

Richard's poker skills were *extraordinary*.

EXTEND (ik-stend) *v.* to draw out to the fullest length

Sally's ballet teacher was impressed with how far she could *extend* her legs.

EXTOL (ik-stohl) *v.* to praise highly

Mrs. Swan *extolled* Sarah's good nature to her parents during their conference.

F

FACET (fas-it) *n.* one small aspect or piece of a subject

There are many *facets* to most people's personalities.

FACTION (fak-shuhn) *n.* a small group within a larger group of people who have interests that are outside of the larger groups' goals

The small *faction* of boys banded together to skip their gym class.

FALTER (fawl-ter) *v.* to hesitate or waver

Bryn's courage did not *falter* when she was faced with slaying the dragon on her favorite video game.

FAMINE (fa-min) *n.* an extreme food shortage

Ireland, as well as many other countries, have suffered from widespread *famine*.

FANATIC (fuh-nat-ik) *n.* a person with extreme enthusiasm about a specific subject

Dixie was a comic book *fanatic*.

FATIGUE (fuh-teeg) *n.* weariness from mental or physical exertion

Running ten miles caused Gregory to suffer from a great deal of *fatigue*.

FATHOM (fath-uhm) *v.* to understand or comprehend

Beth couldn't *fathom* why her cat kept running away.

FAWN (fawn) *v.* to behave affectionately towards

The monkeys in the zoo *fawned* over their new pet kitten.

FAUX (foh) *adj.* artificial or imitation; fake

Michelle's bracelet was made of *faux* pearls.

FEIGN (feyn) *v.* to pretend or make believe

Joey loved to *feign* that he was a pirate.

Nancy *feigned* as if she was sick so she wouldn't have to go to school.

FELINE (fee-lahyn) *adj.* cat-like

Danielle's *feline* agility made her win her gymnastics competition.

FERVOR (fur-ver) *n.* great intensity of emotion

John delivered his debate class speech with *fervor*.

FICKLE (fik-uhl) *adj.* not constant; always changing

Carrie is frustrated by *fickle* changes in weather.

FIDDLE (fid-l) *v.* to play around or waste time

If you *fiddle* around too much in the morning you'll be late for school.

FIDELITY (fi-del-i-tee) *n.* strict loyalty or faithfulness

The politician's *fidelity* to his country was unquestionable.

FINESSE (fi-ness) *n.* skill in handling difficult or impossible situations

Jane had a certain *finesse* for dealing with her angry grandmother.

FLIMSY (flim-zee) *adj.* weak or ineffective

Mary's jacket was too *flimsy* to keep her from getting cold.

FLIPPANT (flip-uhnt) *adj.* disrespectful

Chelsea was sent to the principal's office for being *flippant* during gym class.

FLOURISH (flur-ish) *v.* to decorate or embellish

The baker added many unique flourishes to the wedding cake.

FLUMMOXED (fluhm-uks-ed) *adj.* confused or bewildered

Kari was *flummoxed* by her math homework.

FOE (foh) *n.* an enemy

Outside of Jenny's tree house was a sign that read, "friend or *foe*?"

Laziness is a *foe* to good health.

FOIL (foil) *v.* to prevent the success of someone or something

John had plans to *foil* Max's birthday part because he had not been invited.

FOREMOST (fawr-mohst) *adj.* first in order, place, importance, or rank

The *foremost* thing on Mike's mind was finding somewhere to eat breakfast.

Discussing the new business plan was the manager's *foremost* concern.

FORFEIT (fawr-fit) *v.* to loose as a consequence of a fault or mistake

Samantha's soccer team had to *forfeit* the game because too many players tardy.

FORGERY (fawr-juh-ree) *n.* the illegal reproduction of something, such as a painting, signature, or book

Jake's *forgery* of his father's signature was totally obvious.

FORGO (fawr-goh) *v.* to go without or give up

Lee decided to *forgo* buying a new pair of shoes so that she could buy a dress instead.

FORSAKEN (fawr-sey-ken) *adj.* abandoned or deserted

Lily did not want to sleep in the old *forsaken* barn because she thought it would be haunted.

FORTUITOUS (fawr-too-i-tuhs) *adj.* fortunate or lucky

It was *fortuitous* that the travelers found a gas station just before they ran out of gas.

FOUL (foul) *adj.* unfavorable or unpleasant

Joey had to put his shirt over his nose to avoid the *foul* smell.

FRAUD (frawd) *n.* a person who deceives others for their own gain

The man on the telephone selling pet insurance was obviously a *fraud*.

FRIGID (frij-id) *adj.* very cold in temperature

The snowfall made the morning air *frigid*.

FUTILE (fyoot-il) *adj.* totally ineffective; useless

The stranded tourists started to think that getting back to their hotel was a *futile* idea.

G

GALLANT (gal-uhnt) *adj.* brave or chivalrous

The *gallant* knight rescued the princess from the mean dragon.

GALLIVANT (gal-uh-vant) *v.* to wander about in search of pleasure

The group of tourists *gallivanted* all over the city.

GALLOWS (gal-ohz) *n.* pl. a wooden frame on which condemned people are executed by being hanged

The criminal committed an act so horrible that he earned his place on the *gallows*.

GAPE (geyp) *v.* to stare in wonder usually with an open mouth

Pail couldn't help but *gape* when he saw his neighbor's dog riding a bicycle.

GARNISH (gahr-nish) *v.* to add something that provides color, flavor, or decoration

Mrs. Kim liked to *garnish* her eggs with paprika.

GENERIC (juh-ner-ik) *adj.* general; unspecific

Adam took the *generic* version of the pain reliever because it worked just as well and wasn't as expensive.

GENOCIDE (jen-uh-sahyd) *n.* the deliberate extermination of a national, racial, or cultural group

The mass *genocide* of the Jews during World War II was beyond horrific.

GIBBERISH (jib-er-ish) *n.* meaningless talk or writing

Jake thought it was funny to talk *gibberish* with his best friend Samantha.

GILDED (gild-ed) *adj.* coated with gold

John gave Hilary a *gilded* ring for her birthday.

GLOAT (gloht) *v.* to feel or express arrogant self-satisfaction

Only those with very poor manners *gloat* over someone else's misfortune.

GLUTTON (gluht-n) *n.* a person who eats or drinks excessively

Professor Williams warned his students against becoming *gluttons*.

GOATEE (goh-tee) *n.* a man's beard trimmed to a point on the chin

Instead of a mustache, Mark decided to grow a *goatee*.

GORE (gohr) *n.* bloodshed; bodily damage shown in detail

Gregory hated the movie because it had way too much *gore*.

GORGE (gawrj) *v.* to stuff with food

Amanda loved to *gorge* herself on every holiday.

GOUGE (gouj) *v.* to dig or force out

Barry painfully *gouged* the sliver from his finger.

GOUT (gout) *n.* a disease characterized by the inflammation of the joints especially in the hands and feet

Henry VIII suffered from very painful *gout*.

GRAVE (greyv) *adj.* serious or solemn

The consequences of robbery are very *grave*.

GRIMACE (grim-uhs) *n.* an ugly facial expression that indicates pain or displeasure

Mrs. Daniels had a *grimaced* after eating far too much cake.

GROSS (grohs) *adj.* disgusting or offensive

Connie thinks that seafood is *gross*.

Meredith has gross *table* manners.

GRUFF (gruhf) *adj.* low and harsh; hoarse

Mary's voice sounded *gruff* because of her sore throat.

Jim had a *gruff* attitude on the playground.

GUILE (gahyl) *n.* cunning or crafty deception

Sally played the game with *guile* which, although unpleasant, helped her win.

GULLIBLE (guhl-uh-buhl) *adj.* easily tricked or cheated

Brad is so *gullible* that he'll believe anything you tell him.

GUST (guhst) *n.* a sudden burst of wind

Nate was blown over by a strong *gust* of wind.

GUSTO (guhs-toh) *n.* hearty enjoyment in doing something

The groom spoke to his wedding guests with *gusto*.

GYRATE (jahy-reyt) *v.* to move around in a circle

Derek laughed while everyone *gyrated* on the dance floor.

H

HAIL (heyl) *v.* where someone comes from; place of home or birth

William told his friends that his grandparents *hailed* from England.

HALLOWED (hal-ohd) *adj.* regarded as holy

Churches are more often than not seen as *hallowed* places.

HALLUCINATE (huh-loo-suh-neyt) *v.* to see or perceive what is not there; have illusions

After getting hit on the head with a baseball, Jason began to *hallucinate*.

HAMPER (ham-per) *v.* to hold back or hinder

Freddy didn't want to *hamper* his best friend's chance of getting onto the baseball team.

HAPLESS (hap-lis) *adj.* unfortunate; unlucky

Breaking his grandmother's favorite vase was just one of the many *hapless* events George experienced while house-sitting.

HAZARDOUS (haz-er-dous) *adj.* full of risk; dangerous

It can be *hazardous* to go skydiving.

HEATHEN (hee-thuhn) *n.* an uncivilized person

Heather was convinced that the children she babysat for were *heathens*.

HEARTY (hahr-tee) *adj.* substantial and abundant

Jeremy ordered a *hearty* stack of pancakes for breakfast.

HEAVE (heev) *v.* to throw with force

Christopher *heaved* the anchor overboard.

HEED (heed) *v.* to pay close attention to

It's always wise to *heed* your doctor's advice.

HEIRLOOM (air-loom) *n.* a family possession handed down from generation to generation

Cindy told her friends that the necklace she was wearing was an *heirloom* from her grandmother.

HEIST (hahyst) *n.* a holdup or robbery

Luckily, no one was hurt during the string of bank *heists*.

HERALD (her-uhld) *n.* an official messenger

The king sent his *heralds* to discuss the war with the general.

HESITATE (hez-i-teyt) *v.* to wait to act because of fear

Emily *hesitated* before she crossed the street.

HOARD (hawrd) *v.* to save or collect in a greedy manner

Jan decided to *hoard* her pennies for a rainy day.

HOAX (hohks) *n.* something intended to deceive

There was much debate over the authenticity of the pirate map, so it was not surprising that it turned out to be a *hoax*.

HOMAGE (hom-ij) *n.* to pay respect or reverence

The speech paid *homage* to the civil rights activists.

HONE (hohn) *v.* to sharpen or improve your skills

If Angela wanted to be part of the school musical she was going to have to *hone* her dance skills.

HORIZONTAL (hawr-uh-zon-tl) *adj.* level or flat to the ground

Mrs. Bumble told us all to lie down *horizontally* so that we could play a game.

HOSIERY (hoh-zhuh-ree) *n.* socks or stockings or any kind

Danielle couldn't leave her house without wearing some kind of *hosiery*.

HOSTILE (hos-tl) *adj.* aggressively unfriendly

Susan was upset by the *hostile* greeting she received at her brother's house.

HUMBLE (huhm-buhl) *adj.* not proud or arrogant

When receiving a compliment it is best to be *humble* but appreciative.

HYPOCRITE (hip-uh-krit) *n.* a person who fakes having desirable qualities, but doesn't actually practice the qualities in their private life

When they found out about the scandal, the town thought that their mayor was a total *hypocrite*.

HYSTERICAL (his-ter-i-kuhl) *adj.* emotionally uncontrollable

Marie was *hysterical* after her goldfish died.

I

IDEAL (ahy-deel) *adj.* characterized by excellence and perfection

Sleeping on a blow-up mattress in a closet is not *ideal*.

IDENTICAL (ahy-den-ti-kuhl) *adj.* exactly the same

The twins were *identical* in every way but their hair color.

IDIOM (id-ee-uhm) *n.* a language or style of speaking associated with a particular group of people

Poets and writers often have a different kind of *idiom* than other people.

IGNORAMUS (ig-nuh-rey-muhs) *n.* an extremely ignorant or stupid person

Sometimes Jeffery couldn't help being such an *ignoramus*.

ILLEGIBLE (i-lej-uh-buhl) *adj.* impossible to read due to poor handwriting

Mrs. Tatum couldn't grade Zach's homework because his handwriting is *illegible*.

IMMACULATE (i-mak-yuh-lit) *adj.* free from stains or dirt

The hotel was known for its *immaculate* bed sheets.

IMMUNITY (i-myoo-ni-tee) *n.* the state of being insusceptible to harm

Winning the challenge on the reality TV game show offered the contestant *immunity* from losing.

IMPAIR (im-pair) *v.* to make worse

More often than not, bad weather conditions *impair* peoples' ability to see while they're driving.

IMPRACTICAL (im-prak-ti-kuhl) *adj.* not useful or practical

The dress Sarah bought to wear to the prom was totally *impractical*.

It was *impractical* for Jeff to drive back and forth to work three times in one day.

IMPRESSIONABLE (im-presh-uh-nuh-buhl) *adj.* capable of being easily impressed

Catherine learned to dance at an *impressionable* age.

IN LIEU (en-loo) *prep.* instead of or in something's place

In lieu of flowers, Candace made a donation to a charity.

Janice ate a brownie *in lieu* of a cupcake.

INADMISSIBLE (in-uhd-mis-uh-buhl) *adj.* not allowed or admissible

The evidence in the trial was ruled to be *inadmissible*.

INCARCERATE (en-kahr-suh-reyt) *v.* to imprison

The kidnapper has been *incarcerated* for five years.

INCENTIVE (in-sen-tiv) *n.* a reward or something that provokes to increased productivity

As an *incentive* to get good grades, Mrs. Beach offered her son a gift when he brought home a good report card.

INCLINATION (in-kluh-ney-shuhn) *n.* a tendency to lean towards a certain condition or action

Michael had an *inclination* to go out for Italian food rather than cook pasta at home.

INCOGNITO (in-kog-nee-toh) *adj.* having a concealed identity, or being in disguise

Amber's unicorn Halloween costume allowed her to attend the party *incognito*.

INCOHERENT (in-koh-heer-uhnt) *adj.* without logical connection

Brian was so tired that he wasn't making sense and all his sentences seemed *incoherent*.

INDECIPHERABLE (in-di-sahy-fer-uh-buhl) *adj.* not understandable or illegible

To people who don't speak it, French in an *indecipherable* language.

The handwriting on the note was completely *indecipherable*.

INDEFINITE (in-def-uh-nit) *adj.* not defined or determined

The time that the party actually started was *indefinite*.

INDICT (in-dahyt) *v.* to charge with an offense or crime

Barney was *indicted* with kidnapping Mr. Black's poodle.

INDIFFERENT (in-dif-er-uhnt) *adj.* not concerned or not caring

James was *indifferent* about the football game.

INEDIBLE (in-ed-uh-buhl) *adj.* unfit to be eaten; disgusting

The fish from the market was so rotten that it was *inedible*.

INEPT (in-ept) *adj.* without skill

When it came to playing fetch, Lisa's dog was completely *inept*.

INFAMOUS (in-fuh-muhs) *adj.* having a very bad reputation for something

Charles was an *infamous* flirt.

Bonnie and Clyde were *infamous* bank robbers.

INFINITE (in-fuh-nit) *adj.* unlimited or immeasurable

Dallas wished that the world had an *infinite* supply of cotton candy.

INFLICT (in-flikt) *v.* to impose anything unwelcome

The restaurant was so popular that its customers were often *inflicted* with a long wait to eat.

INHABIT (in-hab-it) to live in a place

Patrick had *inhabited* his apartment for the last three years.

INHERIT (in-her-it) *v.* to receive something from someone else

Jimmy *inherited* his father's eyes.

Ben was happy to *inherit* a fortune from his grandfather.

INITIAL (i-nish-uhl) *adj.* occurring at the start or beginning; first

Hillary's *initial* plan was to eat a snack before she did her math homework.

INNATE (i-neyt) *adj.* having always existed in someone or something

Mozart was said to have an *innate* musical talent.

INNOVATE (in-uh-veyt) *v.* to make something new

The company was *innovative* with its new designs.

INSATIABLE (in-sey-shuh-buhl) *adj.* incapable of being appeased or satisfied

Sierra's appetite for pineapple is *insatiable*.

INSIGHT (in-sayht) *n.* a gained understanding of a situation that helps to solve a problem

Matilda gained a lot of *insight* about her brother's behavior after spending a few hours with his friends.

INSINUATE (in-sin-yoo-yet) *v.* to hint or suggest

Buffy *insinuated* that she would like her room-mate to go with her to the movies.

INSIPID (in-sip-id) *adj.* boring; uninteresting

Hearing the same story over and over again is *insipid*.

INSISTENT (in-sis-tuhnt) *adj.* persistently demanding

Jane was *insistent* that her sister check to see if all the doors to the house were locked before they left to go to shopping.

INSTINCTUALLY (in-sting-k-choo-al-ee) ad*v.* something that happens automatically or naturally

Brenda *instinctually* ran away when the dog started growling at her.

INSURMOUNTABLE (in-ser-moun-tuh-buhl) *adj.* incapable of being overcome

Napoleon's army was not as *insurmountable* as he had thought it was.

INTENSIVE (in-ten-siv) *adj.* pertaining to or characterized by intensity

Mark chose to take the advanced French class because it was more *intensive*.

INTERJECT (in-ter-jekt) *v.* to insert between or come between

Rob *interjected* with an argument before his father had finished.

INTERROGATE (in-ter-uh-geyt) *v.* to examine with questions

Bob was *interrogated* by a police officer about his car accident.

INTERVENE (in-ter-veen) *v.* to interrupt an argument or fight

The ambassador had to *intervene* between the two warring countries.

INTOXICATE (in-tok-si-keyt) *v.* to excite or influence someone in a manner that results in diminished physical and mental control

Before her date Melissa sprayed on a lot of perfume to try and *intoxicate* her date.

INTROVERTED (in-troh-vert-ed) *adj.* shy and reserved

Malcolm has always been slightly more *introverted* than the rest of his family.

IRK (urk) *v.* to annoy or irritate

Mr. Johnson was *irked* when he found that his flowers had been stomped all over by the neighborhood children.

IRONY (ahy-ruh-nee) *n.* the use of words to mean the opposite of the literal meaning of the words used

William Shakespeare's plays are full of *irony*.

IRRELEVANT (i-rel-uh-vuhnt) *adj.* not important or meaningful to a concern

David thought that his sister's comments were totally *irrelevant*.

IRREPARABLE (i-rep-er-uh-buhl) *adj.* not able to be fixed

The storm had caused *irreparable* damage to the barn's roof.

ITINERARY (ahy-tin-uh-rer-ee) *n.* a detailed plan for a journey; a list of places to visit; plan of travel

The tour's *itinerary* for Monday included a light breakfast, followed by a brisk jogging tour of the royal gardens.

J

JARGON (jahr-gun) *n.* the language associated with any particular group or trade; confusing, meaningless talk

Although Mr. Brown was trying to make himself understood what he was saying sounded to most like complete *jargon*.

Dr. Holmes often spoke in medical *jargon*.

JEOPARDY (jep-er-dee) *n.* peril or danger

Jaden was in *jeopardy* of failing her English class.

JOVIAL (joh-vee-uhl) *adj.* characterized by good humor; having a sense of lively joy

The New Year's party was very *jovial*

JOUST (joust) *v.* to participate in combat involving two horses in which each opponent tries to knock the other off of their horse

Jousting was a popular pastime for many knights.

K

KERFUFFLE (ker-fuh-fel) *n.* disorder or some kind of commotion

After baking cupcakes, Molly found her kitchen was a complete *kerfuffle*.

KOWTOW (kou-tou) *v.* to act in a submissive or servile way

It upset Rita to have to *kowtow* to her new boss.

KUDOS (koo-dohs) *n.* pl. statements of praise

The chickens gave each other *kudos* for crossing the street safely.

L

LABYRINTH (lab-uh-rinth) *n.* a difficult maze of paths and passageways in which it's difficult to find a way out

Peter set up a *labyrinth* made of sheets in his front yard for the trick-or-treaters on Halloween.

LACERATION (las-uh-rey-shuhn) *n.* a cut or wound

David needed twenty stitches because of his *laceration*.

LAMENT (luh-ment) *v.* to feel or express sorrow

Dean *lamented* the loss of his pet hamster.

LAPSE (laps) *n.* a trivial error or slip

Miriam suffered from a short period of memory *lapse*.

LAUDABLE (law-duh-buhl) *adj.* deserving praise

Reorganizing Becky's closet was a *laudable* idea.

LAVISH (lav-ish) *adj.* characterized by extravagance

The wedding guests ate a *lavish* dinner followed by wedding cake.

LAX (laks) *adj.* not severe or strict

Michael's boss at work was very *lax*.

LEGACY (leg-uh-see) *n.* something handed down from the past

William's grandfather left him a *legacy* of leather-bound books.

LENIENT (lee-nee-uhnt) *adj.* laid-back; permissive

Will was very *lenient* when it came to disciplining his dog.

LEST (lest) *conj.* for fear that

Leslie took a lot of notes *lest* she might forget something important.

LEVEE (lev-ee) *n.* an embankment designed to keep a river from flooding

The children were warned not to play near the *levee*.

LIAISON (lee-ey-zawn) *n.* a person who serves to maintain communication or contact with two separate groups

Jeff hated being a *liaison* between his parents when they fought with each other.

LIBERATED (lib-uh-reyt-ed) *adj.* to be let free

The prisoners of war were *liberated* when the peace treaty had finally been signed.

LIMB (lim) *n.* an extension or projecting part of an animal, such as an arm or leg or a larger tree branch

Jessica was surprised at how far Frank could stretch his *limbs*.

Fred was sad when a *limb* of his favorite tree had to be cut off.

LIMBO (lim-boh) *n.* a midway state or place

Nan found herself in *limbo* on who she should vote for.

LISTLESS (list-lis) *adj.* lacking energy or not wanting to exert any energy

Katherine felt *listless* after her gym class.

LITERAL (lit-er-uhl) *adj.* the strict or actual meaning of a word

Martha took every word that her teacher said about getting into a good college *literally*.

Debby did not understand the *literal* translation she'd read of the French poem.

LIVID (liv-id) *adj.* furiously angry; enraged

Marnie was *livid* when she found out that her backpack had been stolen from her locker.

LOAF (lohf) *v.* to lounge or move around lazily

Debra would be perfectly happy to spend her weekends *loafing* around her kitchen.

LOATHE (lohth) *v.* to hate or feel extreme dislike for something

Sylvia obviously *loathed* broccoli.

LOCALE (loh-kal) *n.* a place or location

The movie director found a scary *locale* to film the scene.

LONGEVITY (lon-jev-i-tee) *n.* a long span of time, or a long lifetime

Julia's grandmother was known for her *longevity*.

LOOT (loot) *n.* a collection of valued objects or treasure

Becky was very pleased with the *loot* she received at birthday party.

LUCRATIVE (loo-kra-tiv) *adj.* profitable; moneymaking

Meadow was up to another one of her *lucrative* schemes.

LULL (luhl) *v.* to soothe

Jess *lulled* her little sister to sleep with a lullaby.

LUMINOUS (loo-muh-nuhs) *adj.* illuminated or reflecting a lot of light

Sarah's eyes always look so pretty and *luminous*.

LUNATIC (loo-nuh-tik) *n.* an insane person

Fanny was acting like a complete *lunatic* after she found out she won the baking contest.

LUNGE (luhnj) *v.* to thrust forward

Perry *lunged* with a sword during his fencing practice.

LURCH (lurch) *v.* to move forward awkwardly and suddenly

The taxi *lurched* in front of the house.

LURE (loor) *v.* to attract or entice

Mr. Henry's cat was *lured* back to the house with a can of tuna fish.

LYNCH (linch) *v.* to put to death by hanging without the permission of the law

The sheriff was not in time to stop the accused bank robbers of being *lynched*.

M

MACHO (mah-cho) *adj.* having qualities that are considered manly

David always acts very *macho* when he's watching football.

MAKESHIFT (meyk-shift) *adj.* suitable as a temporary substitute for something more permanent

Tommy built a *makeshift* tent out of a sheet and some sticks.

MALICE (mal-is) *n.* the desire to inflict pain or injury on another person

Despite her normally sweet nature, Jamie couldn't help but feel a little *malice* towards her noisy neighbors.

MALIGNANT (muh-lig-nuhnt) *adj.* dangerous or harmful

Cancer cells are *malignant*.

MANGY (meyn-gee) *adj.* scruffy or shabby

Nicholas decided to pet the dog even though it looked totally *mangy*.

MANICURED (man-i-kyoor-ed) *adj.* trimmed and well taken care of

Polly's fingernails were often *manicured*.

Daphne had a very well-*manicured* lawn.

MANIFESTATION (man-uh-fuh-stey-shuhn) *n.* a materialization of an idea or thing

At first there was no clear *manifestation* of Grace's chicken pox until she started to break out into spots.

MANIPULATE (man-i-pew-late) *v.* to control in a skillful manner

The puppeteer *manipulated* the marionette so well that his movements were indistinguishable from those of a real person.

MANSLAUGHTER (man-slaw-ter) *n.* the killing of a human being by another human being; murder

The murderer had been convicted of *manslaughter* in a court of law.

MANUAL (man-yoo-uhl) *adj.* done by hand or human effort

Mrs. Norris did some *manual* labor in her backyard by pulling out the weeds in her garden.

MARTIAL LAW (mar-shawl lawh) *n.* the law enforced by military forces when a government has broken down

Martial law usually takes away the rights held by ordinary citizens.

MARVEL (mahr-vuhl) *v.* to be curious or wonder about something

Ted *marveled* at the sky and wondered how many stars there actually were.

MATERNAL (muh-tur-nl) *adj.* having the qualities of a mother

Even though she had no children of her own, Greg's aunt was very *maternal*.

MATRIARCH (mey-tree-ahrk) *n.* the female head of a family or group

Mrs. Williams was proud to be her family's oldest *matriarch*.

MECCA (mek-uh) *n.* a place that is considered the center of interest or activity

Many consider Paris to be a *Mecca* for artists.

MEDIA (mee-dee-uh) *n.* the means of communication, such as newspapers, television, or radio, that supplies information to a wide amount of people

The *media* covered the president's speech.

MEDITATE (med-i-teyt) *v.* to contemplate or reflect; to think about something deeply

Amy *meditated* on the subject of beauty for a long time.

MEDLEY (med-lee) a mixture of something

Jessica's smoothie contained a *medley* of fruit.

MELEE (mey-ley) *n.* a confused jumble of things

There was a *melee* of presents on the table after the wedding.

Eric had a *melee* of things mixed in his health shake.

MEMENTO (muh-men-toh) *n.* an object that reminds someone of a person or event; a keepsake

Bridget took a seashell from the beach as a *memento*.

MENACE (men-is) *n.* something or someone that threatens to cause harm or injury.

Janice scolded her son for being such a *menace* at school.

MENACINGLY (men-is-ing-lee) *adv.* acting in a way that is threatening or annoying

Nicole *menacingly* stomped up the stairs to her bedroom after she'd been grounded.

MENTOR (men-tawr) *n.* a wise and trusted teacher

Liam was very sad when he learned that his first *mentor* had died.

Andrew was pleased to be learning from such a brilliant *mentor*.

MERIT (mer-it) *n.* something that deserves consideration or praise

The song wasn't Beth's favorite but she agreed that it deserved recognition and *merit*.

MIMIC (mim-ik) *v.* to copy or imitate

The twins started to *mimic* each other so that no one could tell them apart.

MIRAGE (mi-rahzh) *n.* an illusion

The pool appeared like a *mirage* in the desert.

MODEST (mod-ist) *adj.* not proud or boastful; not too showy

Mr. Anderson warmly welcomed us into his *modest* home.

MOMENTUM (moh-men-tuhm) *n.* force or speed of movement

The plane gained *momentum* before it took off into the sky.

MONARCHY (mon-er-kee) *n.* supreme power held by one person, such as a king or queen or the country that is ruled by one person

Queen Elizabeth II is the head of the English *monarchy*.

MONSOON (mon-soon) *n.* a season of heavy rainfall

It isn't very wise to fly a kite in a *monsoon*.

MONSTROSITY (mon-stos-i-tee) *n.* something resembling a monster or the character of being monstrous

Getting braces on her teeth made Barbara feel like she was some kind of *monstrosity*.

MORBID (mawr-bid) *adj.* suggesting an unhealthy mental state; unnaturally gloomy

Angel had a *morbid* obsession with death.

MOTIVE (moh-tiv) *n.* something that encourages a person to act in a certain way; an incentive

Getting into a good school was one of Harriet's biggest *motives* for studying so hard.

MUSTER (muh-ster) *v.* to gather or rouse

Bob *mustered* all his courage before he went into the boxing ring.

MUTATE (myoo-teyt) *v.* to change

The monster's face started to *mutate* when the moon came up.

MUTINY (myoot-n-ee) *n.* rebellion against an authority

The sailors on the ship committed *mutiny* against their captain.

MYTH (mith) *n.* an imaginary person or story

The legend of Bigfoot is a *myth*.

N

NAVIGATE (nav-i-geyt) *v.* to find one's way or give directions

Jerry *navigated* the best way to get through traffic.

NEMESIS (nem-uh-sis) *n.* an opponent or rival; an enemy

Although his *nemesis* escaped, the hero felt he had still triumphed.

NEWFOUND (noo-found) *adj.* newly discovered or found

Frank wasn't sure why he had a *newfound* interest in chess.

NICHE (nich) *n.* a small place or position

Darren hid his favorite rock in a little *niche*.

Rhoda found her *niche* in the business world.

NOCTURNAL (nok-tur-nl) *adj.* anything to do with the nighttime

Koala bears are *nocturnal* animals.

NOMAD (noh-mad) *n.* a wanderer; someone with no permanent home

Neanderthals were a *nomadic* people.

NOMINATE (nom-uh-neyt) *v.* to appoint someone to a job or duty

Nathan *nominated* his best friend to be the president of the star gazing club.

NONCHALANT (non-shuh-lahnt) *adj.* unconcerned, indifferent, or cool; not worried

Fred walked into the party with a *nonchalant* attitude.

NORMALCY (nawr-muhl-see) *n.* the quality of being normal

Doing the dishes after dinner every night gave John a sense of *normalcy*.

NOTEWORTHY (noht-wur-thee) *adj.* worthy of attention

Melanie's good manners were very *noteworthy*.

NOVEL (nov-uhl) *adj.* different from anything seen before; new

The song about ponies introduced a *novel* new kind of music.

NOVICE (nov-is) *n.* a person who is new to circumstances like work or a hobby

Although she was very good at chess, Monica was still considered a *novice*.

O

OASIS (oh-ey-sis) a pleasant refuge from the usual

Sam thought that his grandma's house was an *oasis*.

OBESE (oh-bees) *adj.* overweight

There should be laws to prohibit the discrimination of *obese* people.

OBJECTION (uhb-jek-shuhn) *n.* a reason for argument

The lawyer made an *objection* when the witness didn't tell the full truth.

OBLIGATION (ob-li-gey-shuhn) *n.* something that has to be done due to a promise, contract, or sense of duty

Calvin fulfilled his *obligation* of cleaning out the garage.

OBLIGED (uh-blahyj-ed) *v.* to be indebted or grateful

Courtney was much *obliged* to her friend for the ride home from school.

OBLITERATE (uh-blit-uh-reyt) *v.* to remove all traces of something; to erase

The forest was *obliterated* by new housing developments.

OBLIVIOUS (uh-bliv-ee-uhs) *adj.* unaware or unconscious

Anne was *oblivious* of how her mood affected the other people around her.

OBSERVER (uhb-zur-ver) *n.* someone who watches or observes

The *observer* watched while Mrs. Norris taught her class.

Jen noticed that she had an *observer* watching her every move.

OBSCURE (uhb-skyoor) *v.* to conceal or confuse

The poet hid the true meaning of the poem by *obscuring* it with many pleasant images.

OBSOLETE (ob-suh-leet) *adj.* no longer in use

Some people think that computers made typewriters *obsolete*.

OBTRUSIVE (uhb-troo-siv) *adj.* showing a disposition to impose yourself and your opinions on others

Janet couldn't stand her *obtrusive* neighbors.

OMEN (oh-muhn) *n.* anything that is seen to be a sign of good or bad luck in events to come

Colby looked at the red robin as a good *omen*.

OMINOUS (om-uh-nuhs) *adj.* threatening

The dark clouds overhead were very *ominous* looking.

OMIT (oh-mit) *v.* to leave out or not include

Claire thought it was a good idea to *omit* the complete truth about what had happened with the stolen books.

Dan *omitted* the fact that he had a crush on Ellie.

OMNIPOTENT (om-nip-uh-tuhnt) *adj.* having unlimited power and knowledge

Whenever Paul put on his superhero costume he felt *omnipotent*.

OPAQUE (oh-peyk) *adj.* not see-through

Opaque, pink tights were required to be worn during Selma's ballet classes.

OPTIMISM (op-tuh-miz-uhm) *n.* a believe that good always triumphs over bad in the world

Nick's *optimism* on the subject of world peace was refreshing.

ORATE (aw-reyt) *v.* to speak or declaim

Ben could *orate* on the subject of libraries for hours and hours.

ORNATE (awr-neyt) *adj.* Elaborately, heavily, and often excessively ornamented

Ellen's wedding dress was very *ornate*.

Tom had an *ornate* way of speaking.

ORTHODOX (awr-thuh-doks) *adj.* customary or conventional

Felicity argued with her father about his *orthodox* view of politics.

OSTRACIZE (os-truh-sahyz) *v.* to exclude from a group; to tease or make fun of

Mary's friends started to *ostracize* her after she embarrassed herself in the lunchroom.

OVERWHELM (oh-ver-welm) *v.* to be completely overcome in your mind and your feelings.

Bridget was *overwhelmed* by the sadness she felt when her cat died.

OUTLANDISH (out-lan-dish) *adj.* very strange or odd

Dressing like a ghost on days other than Halloween is a bit *outlandish*.

OZONE LAYER (oh-zohn ley-er) *n.* a layer of the upper atmosphere that helps protect the earth from the radiation from the sun

Many scientists have stated that the *Ozone Layer* is very important.

P

PACE (peys) *v.* to walk back and forth nervously

The father-to-be *paced* back and forth in the hospital waiting room.

PACIFIST (pas-uh-fist) *n.* a person who is against violence of any kind

Martin Luther King, Jr. was a famous *pacifist*.

PALE (peyl) *adj.* lacking a lot of color; white

The nurse told Monique that she looked very *pale*.

PALLOR (pal-ler) *n.* an unnatural paleness

There was a strange *pallor* to the hippo's skin while it visited the vet.

PANACHE (puh-nash) *n.* a grand and stylish manner

The actress walked down the red carpet with a great deal of *panache.*

PANDEMONIUM (pan-duh-moh-nee-uhm) *n.* disorder and chaos

There was a *pandemonium* at the concert when the band first stepped onstage.

PANTOMIME (pan-tuh-mahym) *n.* a play in which the actors express themselves without talking by using facial expressions and hand gestures

Cindy thought it would be fun to star in a *pantomime* with all of her friends.

PARALLEL (par-uh-lel, -luhl) *adj.* having the same direction, course, nature, or tendency; corresponding; similar

A *parallel* row of trees lined Gary's driveway.

PARAPLEGIC (par-uh-plee-jik) *n.* a person whose lower limbs have been paralyzed due to spinal disease or injury

Charlotte was worried that her father's injuries would turn him into a *paraplegic.*

PARTICIPATE (pahr-tis-uh-peyt) *v.* to take part in an activity with others

Heather enjoyed *participating* with putting up the decorations for the party.

PARTICULAR (per-tik-yuh-ler) *adj.* pertaining to something specific, like a person, thing, or group.

Jim had a *particular* dislike of sweets.

PASSERBY (pas-er-bahy) *n.* someone who passes by

Spot parked at the *passerby*.

PASSIVE (pas-iv) *adj.* not reacting to something that might be expected to cause an emotional reaction

Patricia was *passive* about her lost kitten.

PATHOLOGICAL (path-uh-loj-i-kuhl) *adj.* involving a mental condition or disease

Brenda was afraid that she was turning into a *pathological* liar because of all the lies she'd been telling to cover up her mistakes.

PATRIARCH (pey-tree-ahrk) *n.* a person regarded as a founder or father of a family or group

George Washington is considered the *patriarch* of the United States of America.

PATRONIZE (pey-truh-nahyz) *v.* to act like you're far above someone; to belittle

The professor was accused of *patronizing* the freshman class.

PAUPER (paw-per) *n.* a poor person; a person without wealth

Phil felt like a *pauper* after he spent all of his savings on a new car.

PECKISH (pek-ish) *adj.* somewhat hungry

Terry ate a granola bar because he was feeling a little *peckish*.

PEER (peer) *n.* a person who is equal in age, ability, background, and social status

Jason joined his *peers* for a game of basketball.

In criminal court cases, you're tried before a jury of your *peers*.

PENDING (pen-ding) *adj.* awaiting decision; unfinished

The administrative decision to require locks on all lockers was still *pending*.

PENSIVE (pen-siv) *adj.* deeply or sadly thoughtful

After his dog died Joseph became extremely *pensive*.

PERIL (per-uhl) *n.* something that may cause injury or harm; danger

The dinosaur exhibit was in *peril* of losing its funding.

PERJURY (pur-juh-ree) *n.* lying under oath

The robber was sentenced to more jail time for not only committing robbery, but for committing *perjury* in court.

PERPENDICULAR (pur-puhn-dik-u-lar) *adj.* straight up and down

When Adam wakes up in the morning his hair is *perpendicular* to his head.

PERSECUTE (pur-si-kyoot) *v.* to annoy or harass consistently

Kat was sick of being *persecuted* by her little sister.

PERSEVERE (pur-suh-veer) *v.* to maintain a purpose even though it may be difficult; to persist

Tabitha *persevered* through her grandmother's funeral despite the fact that it made her very sad.

PERSUADE (pur-sweyd) *v.* to urge someone to do something

Mark *persuaded* his girlfriend to join him for Thanksgiving dinner.

PERTINENT (pur-tn-uhnt) *adj.* pertaining directly to the matter at hand

Fran's opinion about the speaker were quite *pertinent*.

PESSIMISM (pes-uh-miz-uhm) *n.* a tendency to see and concentrate on the bad or undesirable

Jose was depressed by his sister's *pessimism*.

PITCH (pich) *adj.* extremely dark

The closet was *pitch* black without a flashlight.

PITTANCE (pit-ns) *n.* a small amount

Roger considered the raise he got at the end of the year a mere *pittance* because he had expected much more money.

PLACATE (pley-keyt) *v.* to appease or pacify

Joann hated *placating* to her roommate's mood swings.

PLAGIARIST (pley-juh-rist) *n.* someone who uses the thoughts and writings of another author and passes them off as their own work

No one wanted to sit next to John because he was a known *plagiarist*.

PLEA (plee) *n.* an appeal or request

The criminal's *plea* for mercy was denied by the judge.

PLEDGE (plej) *v.* to promise seriously

Suzanne *pledged* to be a volunteer hospital worker.

PLIGHT (plahyt) *n.* an unfavorable or unfortunate situation

Brandon was upset with his *plight* of washing dishes for a whole week.

POMPOUS (pom-puhs) *adj.* characterized by arrogance or a false display of dignity

The commander of the naval ship had a very *pompous* attitude.

PONDER (pon-der) *v.* to think deeply

Henry *pondered* a long time about who to ask to the Valentine's Day dance.

POTENT (poht-nt) *adj.* powerful or mighty

The stove had a rather *potent* odor coming from it.

PRACTITIONER (prak-tish-uh-ner) *n.* a person who practices something specified

In order to be a ninja, one must be a *practitioner* of martial arts.

As a doctor, Jerry is a medical *practitioner*.

PRAGMATIC (prag-ma-tik) *adj.* characterized by a practical point of view

Karen has a very *pragmatic* view of politics.

PRECARIOUS (pri-kair-ee-uhs) *adj.* dependent on circumstances that are beyond one's control

Erica was nervous about her *precarious* living situation in the condemned house.

PREDICAMENT (pri-dik-uh-muhnt) *n.* a difficult or unpleasant situation

Gideon found himself in a very strange *predicament* when he woke up on a pirate ship.

PREDOMINANT (pri-dom-uh-nuhnt) *adj.* Main; prevalent; first-noticed

Daphne's moodiness was her *predominant* personality trait.

PREMATURE (pree-muh-choor) *adj.* happening too soon

The announcement that school would be closed for a week due to construction was *premature*.

PREOCCUPIED (pree-ok-yuh-pahyd) *adj.* previously occupied with thought

Terrance was too *preoccupied* with his favorite comic book to answer his cell phone.

PRESTIGE (pre-steej) *n.* a reputation of being successful by achieving a high rank

The general's *prestige* was noticeable the second he walked into the room.

PREY (prey) *n.* a person or thing that is the victim of a predator

William was determined not to be the *prey* of the school bully.

PRIME (prim) *adj.* best in quality or excellence

George's grandfather was constantly saying that he was in the *prime* of his life.

PRIOR (prahy-er) *adj.* happening before; preceding

Jacob's *prior* girlfriend had red hair.

PRISTINE (pris-teen) *adj.* fresh and clean

Tisha loved the *pristine* smell of a new pair of socks.

PROCEEDS (proh-seeds) *n.* pl. profits or returns from a sale or business transaction

All of the *proceeds* from the bake sale were donated to charity.

PROSCRASTINATE (proh-kras-tuh-neyt) *v.* to delay

Gustave *procrastinated* doing his homework so that he could watch the tennis match.

PRODIGAL (prod-i-guhl) *adj.* extravagantly wasteful

Emily was often *prodigal* with her allowance.

PROFUSE (pruh-fyoos) *adj.* a great amount; abundant

It was obvious that Nikki had spent a *profuse* amount on her new school wardrobe.

PROPAPGANDA (prop-uh-gan-duh) *n.* information deliberately spread to help or harm a person, group, or institution

Vikki didn't listen to the politician's negative *propaganda.*

PROSAIC (proh-zey-ik) *adj.* matter-of-fact and unoriginal

The book was written in a *prosaic* manner which made it very dull to read.

PROSE (prohz) *n.* the ordinary form of written and spoken language

Pete was praised for his journalistic *prose.*

PROTRUDE (proh-trood) *v.* to stick out or thrust forward

Tony's fishing pole *protruded* from his bag.

PROVINCIAL (pruh-vin-shuhl) *adj.* a person who lacks open-mindedness and sophistication

Although Billy was from the country his manners were far from *provincial.*

PROXIMITY (prok-sim-i-tee) *n.* nearness in place or time

These tragic events happened in strange *proximity* to one another.

PRY (prahy) *v.* to inquire unnecessarily into other peoples' business.

Nothing is worse than having a nosy neighbor that *pries*.

PSYCHOLOGICAL (sahy-kuh-loj-i-kuhl) *adj.* having to do with what affects the mind

Jenny felt like she might have a *psychological* breakdown if she didn't get asked to the dance.

Q

QUANDARY (kwon-duh-ree) a state of uncertainty; a dilemma

Joe found himself in a *quandary* when he missed his bus.

QUARREL (kwawr-uhl) *v.* an angry dispute or fight

Brooke couldn't help but overhear her parents *quarrel*.

QUEUE (kyoo) *n.* a line

Laura was in a *queue* for 20 minutes at the supermarket.

QUIBBLE (kwib-uhl) *v.* to find fault and criticize

Albert *quibbled* about the smallest little things.

QUIRK (kwurk) *n.* a strange part of someone's behavior

Harry's *quirk* was wearing stained t-shirts.

R

RADICAL (rad-i-kuhl) *adj.* excellent or wonderful

Karen's skateboarding skills are completely *radical*.

RALLY (ral-ee) *v.* to gather, organize, and inspire

The general *rallied* his troops before they went into battle.

RANT (rant) *n.* a violent or extravagant exclamation or speech

After he was turned down for a loan, Mr. Rodin focused always *ranted* about the bank.

RAPPORT (ra-pawr) *n.* a close and harmonious relationship

Matilda had a great *rapport* with her cousins.

REALISTIC (ree-uhl-is-tik) *adj.* interested in what is real or practical

Mark *realistically* couldn't be in two places at one time.

REAP (reep) *v.* to get in return

April *reaped* the benefits of her hard work by receiving an A in her Math class.

REBUTTAL (ri-buht-l) *n.* a statement made during an argument or debate

Sally presented a *rebuttal* to the statement that cupcakes are good for you.

RECONCILE (rek-uhn-sahyl) *v.* to bring to an agreement or harmony

The sisters *reconciled* their argument over shoes with a delicious lunch.

RECOUNT (ree-kount) *v.* to narrate or relate the facts of a story

Jed decided to *recount* the details of his story to his teacher.

RECTIFY (rek-tuh-fehy) *v.* to set right

Jimmy needed to *rectify* the flat tire on his bicycle.

RECUR (ri-kur) *v.* to happen or occur again

Cybil kept having *recurring* dreams about having a baby.

REDUNDANT (ri-duhn-duhnt) *adj.* characterized by repetition of expressing yourself; saying the same thing; telling the same story over and over again

Phillip hated going to his aunt's house because she always told the same *redundant* story.

REFUGE (ref-yooj) *n.* protection from danger

Marissa took *refuge* underneath her umbrella during the rainstorm.

REHABILITATE (ree-huh-bil-i-teyt) *v.* to restore to good health

Dr. Brown told Ellie to use crutches because her ankle needed to *rehabilitate*.

REKINDLE (ree-kin-duhl) *v.* to renew or revive

They *rekindled* their relationship after ten years.

RELENTLESS (ri-lent-lis) *adj.* persistent and steady

The *relentless* sound of the rain kept Ruby awake all night.

RELEVANT (rel-uh-vuhnt) *adj.* connected to the matter at hand

Jackie made a very *relevant* comment about current events.

RELIEVE (ri-leev) *v.* to ease of any burden

The aspirin Pat took for his headache *relieved* him of his pain.

RELINQUISH (ri-ling-kwish) *v.* to surrender or give up

Rachel *relinquished* the idea that she'd be traveling in Europe all summer because she didn't have enough money to make the trip.

RELUCTANT (ri-luhk-tuhnt) *adj.* unwilling or hesitant

Although she'd been nominated, Elizabeth felt like a *reluctant* candidate for the position.

REMINISCE (rem-uh-nis) *v.* to recall past events and experiences

Andy *reminisced* about the first time he played baseball.

RENDEZVOUS (rahn-duh-voo) *n.* a meeting at a particular time and place

Eric and Cate planned a secret *rendezvous* after school.

RENEGADE (ren-i-geyd) *n.* one who rejects a religion, cause, allegiance, or group for another; a deserter

When Hilary switched schools she was considered a *renegade* by her old friends.

REPENT (ri-pent) *v.* to feel sorry about a past action

Bella felt as if she needed to *repent* for lying to her mother.

REPRESENTATION (rep-ri-zen-tey-shuhn, -zuhn-) *n.* a picture, figure, statue, etc.

Jennifer drew her own *representation* of Leonardo Da Vinci's famous painting, Mona Lisa.

The sculpture was a *representation* of an apple.

REPRIMAND (rep-ruh-mand) *v.* to scold or rebuke

Mr. Hewitt *reprimanded* his students for talking during a test.

REPRIEVE (ri-preev) *n.* temporary relief

The pain medication gave the queen *reprieve* from her painful headache.

REPULSIVE (ri-puhl-siv) *adj.* causing aversion or disgust

Bacon is *repulsive* to many vegetarians.

RESENT (ri-zent) *v.* to be angry because of an insult

Fran *resented* the fact that her brother always teased her and never got in trouble.

RESIGNATION (rez-ig-ney-shuhn) *n.* an accepting and submissive attitude

Ralph accepted being fired from his job with *resignation* rather than anger.

RESOLVE (ri-zohlv) *v.* to determine or decide to do something

Maggie *resolved* to talk to her teacher about her poor grades.

RESOLUTE (rez-uh-loot) *adj.* resolved or determined

Mark was *resolute* that this year he would win the marathon.

RESUME (ri-zoom) *v.* to take up and go again or continue

After dinner, Cheri cleaned the dishes and *resumed* playing her favorite video game.

RETORT (ri-tawrt) *n.* a witty or severe remark that happens after a first speaker's statement

Cynthia tried to think of a *witty* retort after Claude insulted her.

REVEL (rev-uhl) *v.* to celebrate or take great pleasure

Jim *reveled* in his recent success.

REVERE (ri-veer) *v.* to regard with respect

Kari *revered* her grandfather's history.

RIFT (rift) *n.* a break in a friendly relations

The two companies who had worked well together in the past were now experiencing some kind of *rift* because of a miscommunication.

RIGOROUS (rig-er-uhs) *adj.* rigidly accurate; precise

Fran's morning exercise routine was *rigorous*.

RISQUÉ (ri-skey) *adj.* daringly close to being danger-ous or improper

The journalist's opinions about the president were considered to be *risqué*.

RITE (rayht) *n.* a formal, ceremonial, or customary act

Many Christian religions perform the *rites* of baptism.

ROUGE (rooj) *n.* any make-up used for coloring the cheeks or lips

The actress always applied *rouge* so that she would have a cheerful appearance in photographs.

RUSTIC (ruhs-tik) *adj.* unsophisticated, artless, or rural

Many great artists have *rustic* beginnings.

S

SABOTAGE (sab-uh-tahzh) *v.* weakening a cause or interfering with production or work

Denise was accused of *sabotaging* her co-worker's schedule.

Gary *sabotaged* the thieves' getaway by pouring sugar in their car's gas tank.

SATIATED (sey-shee-eyt-ed) *adj.* to be satisfied or full

After her large lobster dinner, Kathy felt com-pletely *satiated*.

SATISFACTORY (sat-is-fak-tuh-ree) *adj.* fulfilling but not exceeding expectations

Doug's performance on the football field was *sat-isfactory*.

SCANTY (skan-tee) *adj.* meager; inadequate

Melissa still felt hungry after her *scanty* meal.

SCOFF (skawf) *v.* to mock

Chuck *scoffed* at his little brother's cartoon lunchbox.

SCUMPTIOUS (skruhmp-shuhs) *adj.* pleasing to the senses

Dallas said that his mother's pineapple cake was simply *scrumptious*.

SCRUPULOUS (skroo-pyuh-luhs) *adj.* showing strict regard for what is considered right and fair

Theo's behavior in the lawsuit against his indecent neighbors was fair and *scrupulous*.

SCRUTINY (skroot-n-ee) *n.* a close and searching look

Agent James looked at the missing necklace case with a lot of *scrutiny*.

SEDENTARY (sed-n-ter-ee) *adj.* accustomed to sitting a lot and exercising very little

Lindsay had a very *sedentary* desk job where she sat and looked at a computer all day.

SEQUENTIAL (si-kwen-shul) *adj.* one following another in a specific order

Monica studied the *sequential* order of the musical notes for her piano lesson.

SERENE (suh-reen) *adj.* calm and peaceful

The view of the ocean from the hotel room was *serene*.

SERVILE (sur-vil) *adj.* pertaining to servitude

Holly found herself working in a *servile* position while working in the lunchroom.

SHREWD (shrood) *adj.* quick and perceptive; intelligent

Thomas considered his grandfather to be a wise and *shrewd* man.

SIESTA (see-es-tuh) *n.* a midday nap; period of relaxation

It is common in Spain to take a *siesta* during the afternoon.

SIMILAR (sim-uh-ler) *adj.* having a likeness in a general way

Angel's shoes were *similar* to Samantha's

SKEPTIC (skep-tik) *n.* someone who often questions the validity or truth of something

Darren couldn't enjoy the magic show because he was such a *skeptic*.

SKIM (skim) *v.* to go over something in a superficial way

The professor just *skimmed* his students' research reports before handing them back.

SKIRMISH (skur-mish) *n.* a small fight

Steven had a *skirmish* with his father about taking out the trash.

SMUGGLE (smuh-gl) *v.* to import or export goods in violation of the law

Nick *smuggled* a bag of licorice to the movie theater because he didn't like the kind the sold at the concession stand.

SOUFFLÉ (soo-fley) *n.* a light baked dish made fluffy with beaten egg whites combined with egg yolks, white sauce, and fish, cheese, or other ingredients

As a surprise for Mother's Day, Jessica made her mother a *soufflé* for lunch.

SOLEMN (sol-uhm) *adj.* grave; sombre

The rabbi made some very *solemn* remarks at the funeral.

SNIDE (snahyd) *adj.* malicious and derogatory

Howard was offended by the *snide* remark that his friend said behind his back.

SPAT (spat) *n.* a small and petty quarrel

When the next door neighbor's Dalmatian dug up Mrs. Roger's flowers, it caused a very long *spat*.

SPONTANEOUS (spon-tey-nee-uhs) *adj.* happening suddenly or impulsively

Donna's *spontaneous* decision to skip her math class and go to the mall instead was unwise.

SQUANDER (skwon-der) *v.* to use extravagantly

Judy *squandered* her time at the ice capades instead of spending it studying.

SQUEAMISH (skwee-mish) *adj.* easily shocked or disgusted

In times of stress Patricia always felt *squeamish*.

SQUINT (skwint) *v.* to look with eyes party closed

James had to *squint* to see because the sun was so bright.

STAGNANT (stag-nuhnt) *adj.* characterized by lack of movement

The pond was starting to smell funny because the water was *stagnant*.

STAMINA (stam-uh-nuh) *n.* the physical ability to endure disease or fatigue; strength

The body builder's *stamina* was really impressive.

STAUNCH (stawnch) *adj.* characterized by firmness or loyalty

Bernie was a *staunch* supporter of the Democratic party.

STRENUOUS (stren-yoo-uhs) *adj.* demanding or requiring a lot of exertion

George's work-out was incredibly *strenuous* but fun.

STUDIOUS (stoo-dee-uhs) *adj.* devoted to studying

Iris was sure to get into a good college because of her *studious* nature.

SUBDUE (suhb-doo) *v.* to overpower by force or bring under control

It was difficult for Gordon to *subdue* his barking dog.

SUBSIDE (sub-sahyd) *v.* to become quiet or less active

The dog's barking *subsided* after it was fed.

SUBSTANCE (suhb-stuhns) *n.* physical or material matte

Tammy mixed glue with paint creating a sticky and colorful *substance*.

SUCCUMB (suh-khum) to yield to a superior force

The king would not *succumb* to the will of his advisors.

SULTRY (suhl-tree) *adj.* really hot and humid

Summer days in New York City can be oppressively *sultry*, especially when riding the subway.

SUPERFICIAL (soo-per-fish-uhl) *adj.* only concerned with what's on the surface

Everyone thought that Diane's view of beauty was totally *superficial*.

SUPERNATURAL (soo-per-nach-er-uhl) *adj.* being beyond what is able to be explained naturally

Ghosts are part of the *supernatural* world.

SUSPICION (suh-spish-uhn) *n.* a notion of something not being right; distrust

Bella had a *suspicion* that Britney was to blame for stealing her lunch.

Melvin's *suspicion* was correct.

SYLLABLE (sil-uh-buhl) *n.* a unit of spoken language consisting of a single sound

When Tony was learning to read he would sound out the *syllables* of each word.

SYMPATHY (sim-puh-thee) *n.* the connection of shared feelings with another person

Linda had a great amount of *sympathy* for the homeless.

SYNONYM (sin-uh-nim) *n.* a word having the same or nearly the same meaning as another word

Happy is a *synonym* for glad.

SYNOPSIS (si-nop-sis) *n.* a brief summary giving a general overview of some subject

Terry's *synopsis* of the book left little to the imagination.

SYNTHETIC (sin-thet-ik) *adj.* artificial; not real or genuine

Mandy's diamond earrings were *synthetic*.

T

TACTIC (tak-tik) *n.* a plan for promoting a desired effect

Mrs. Johnson came up with a good *tactic* to get her son to do his chores.

TAILORED (tey-lerd) *adj.* having a neat or tidy appearance

Tim only wears *tailored* clothing from a fancy store in London.

TANTALIZE (tan-tl-ahyz) *v.* to tease by arousing expectations

Chuck was always *tantalizing* his friends with the promise of chocolate chip cookies.

TARNISH (tahr-nish) *v.* to become dirty; to lose luster

The silver forks Becky inherited from her aunt were *tarnished* with age and wear.

TARTAN (tahr-tun) *adj.* a specific plaid pattern associated with kilts

In Scotland, every clan has a different color and style of *tartan*.

TEDIOUS (tee-dee-uhs) *adj.* boring and dull

Jack thought his piano lessons were *tedious*.

TEMPERATE (tem-per-it) *adj.* not extreme in opinion; moderate

Elaine's thoughts on the matter of new school uniforms were very *temperate*.

THRESHOLD (thresh-ohld) *n.* an entrance or doorway

Austin carried his bride over the *threshold* of their new apartment.

TIMID (tim-id) *adj.* Lacking in confidence or self-assurance; shy

Nancy felt very *timid* before she gave her speech in front of the whole school.

TORMENT (tawr-ment) *v.* to afflict with mental or physical pain

Penny hated the thought that her brother was capable of *tormenting* even a butterfly.

TOXIC (tok-sik) *adj.* having the same effect as poison

Britney thought that her low self-esteem was *toxic*.

TRANSPOSE (tans-pohz) *v.* to change places

Delores wanted to *transpose* her furniture from one side of the room to another.

TRAUMA (traw-muh) *n.* a serious shock or injury to the body

War veterans sometimes suffer from mental *trauma* when they return home.

TRITE (trayht) *adj.* uninteresting because of constant overuse; repetitive; boring

Dan's jokes about his runny nose were starting to became very *trite* very quickly.

TURBULENT (tur-byuh-luhnt) *adj.* characterized by a state of agitation

When she was sleepy Monica's emotions where very *turbulent*.

TYCOON (tahy-koon) *n.* a business person of great power and wealth

Mark was considered as a *tycoon* in the music industry.

U

ULCER (uhl-ser) *n.* any chronic or disrupting condition

Mrs. Ray was so stressed that she was afraid she might soon have a stomach *ulcer*.

ULTERIOR (uhl-teer-ee-er) *adj.* lying beyond an understood boundary

Juan had *ulterior* motives for visiting his father-in-law.

UNANIMOUS (yoo-nan-uh-muhs) *adj.* characterized by complete agreement

The committee's vote to improve the city's water fountains was *unanimous*.

UNAVOIDABLE (uhn-uh-voi-duh-buhl) *adj.* unable to be avoided

Even though she tried to pretend she was sick, Becky's piano lesson was *unavoidable*.

UNBRIDLED (uhn-brahyd-ld) *adj.* free from restraint

The lovers kissed with *unbridled* passion.

UNCONCERNED (uhn-kuhn-surnd) *adj.* unworried or not caring

Sean was *unconcerned* about where to park his car.

UNCONCIOUS (uhn-kon-shuhs) *adj.* without awareness of what is going on around you

Janie was knocked *unconscious* by the baseball that hit her in the head.

UNCOUTH (uhn-kooth) *adj.* having bad manners or being awkward

It was very *uncouth* of Dustin not to pay his part of the dinner bill.

UNDERFOOT (uhn-der-foot) *adj.* lying under the feet

The carpet *underfoot* was starting to get worn.

UNDERMINE (uhn-der-mahyn) to weaken by secret or underhanded means

Julia tried to *undermine* Bill and Jeff's friendship by telling them different lies about each other.

UNDISCLOSED (uhn-dis-klohz-ed) *adj.* not made known

There was a lot of *undisclosed* information that the journalist wanted to know.

UNISON (yoo-nuh-suhn) *n.* a process in which all the elements of something are working at the same time or in the same way

Though it consisted of almost 50 members, the choir sang in *unison*.

UNKEMPT (uhn-kempt) *adj.* messy or uncared for

Lola's room was very *unkempt*.

UNSCRUPULOUS (uhn-skroo-pyuh-luhs) *adj.* without concern for what is right or honorable

Larissa had an *unscrupulous* attitude about getting to work on time.

UNSIGHTLY (uhn-sahyt-lee) *adj.* unpleasant to look at

The garbage on the street gave the neighborhood an *unsightly* appearance.

UPFRONT (uhp-fruhnt) *adj.* straightforward and honest

Alan didn't want to be *upfront* about the stolen crate of lobsters.

UPHEAVAL (uhp-hee-val) *n.* a strong change or disturbance

The *upheaval* of the new attendance system at school confused most of the teachers as well as the students.

UPHOLSTERY (uhp-hohl-stuh-ree) *n.* the materials used to cushion and cover furniture

Jackie decided that it was time to change the *upholstery* on her old sofa.

USURP (yoo-surp) *v.* to seize power without legal permission

> Mary, Queen of Scots was said to have tried to *usurp* her sister's throne.

UTTER (uht-er) *v.* to speak or pronounce something

> Gabe was so shocked he couldn't *utter* a single word after his friends threw him a surprise birthday party.

V

VACATE (vey-keyt) *v.* to give up possession or occupancy

> Keri had to *vacate* her apartment because she could not afford the rent.

VACILLATE (vas-uh-leyt) *v.* to waver in opinion

> Jack *vacillated* between buying a pair of red sneakers or a pair of blue sneakers.

VANDALIZE (van-dl-ahyz) *v.* to destroy of deface property that doesn't belong to you

> The graffiti artist is commonly accused of *vandalizing* public property.

VANQUISH (vang-kwish) *v.* to conquer with superior force

> The evil knight was *vanquished* by the king.

VEGETARIAN (vej-i-tair-ee-uhn) *n.* a person who does not eat meat

> Liz's older sister became a *vegetarian* because she didn't like to eat meat.

VELOCITY (vuh-los-i-tee) *n.* how fast something travels; speed

> Mr. Thomas was having a hard time during his golf game due to the high wind *velocity*.

VEER (veer) *v.* to change direction quickly

When the ball bounced into the street Mr. Field's car *veered* out of the way just in time.

VERBOSE (ver-bohs) *adj.* characterized by the use of too many words

Mrs. Smith was known for her *verbose* speeches on current events.

VERIFY (ver-uh-fey) *v.* to confirm or prove the truth of something

Bradley's co-worker had to *verify* the correct spelling of his last name.

VEX (veks) *v.* to irritate or provoke; to be irritated

Gloria was *vexed* by her flat tire.

VIAL (vahyl) *n.* a small glass container

There were several *vials* of different chemicals on the Chemistry teacher's desk.

VIRULENT (vir-yuh-luhnt) *adj.* violently aggressive

The prize fighter was known for being *virulent* in the boxing ring.

VIVACIOUS (vi-vey-shuhs) *adj.* lively

Kim took part in the *vivacious* hula-hoop contest.

VIVID (viv-id) *adj.* intense; bright

Amber's eyes are a *vivid* blue.

The painting was made with many *vivid* colors.

VOLITION (voh-lish-uhn) *n.* the act of choosing or resolving

After the disagreement Terrance left town on his own *volition*.

VULGAR (vuhl-ger) *adj.* obscene or lewd; indecent or offensive

Julia got in trouble for using *vulgar* language.

VULNERABLE (vuhl-ner-uh-buhl) *adj.* susceptible to injury

The monkey was in quite a *vulnerable* position as he jumped from one lion's head to another.

W

WALLOW (wol-oh) *v.* to give in to a moody or sad state of mind; to roll around in the mud

Sharon didn't want to *wallow*, but couldn't help but be upset about the loss of her goldfish.

WARRANT (wawr-uhnt) *n.* a written document that certifies or gives authority

The police had a *warrant* to search the back of the clown's car.

WAVER (wey-ver) to doubt or go back and forth about a decision

Oliver's opinion about the play *wavered* from good to bad.

WEARY (weer-ee) *adj.* mentally or physically exhausted from hard work

Daniel felt *weary* after a long day of working on his grandfather's farm.

WELD (weld) *v.* to bring together or fuse

Tom *welded* a piece of metal to his newest sculpture.

WELL-BEING (wel-bee-ing) *n.* a good condition of living

Isabel's *well-being* was more important to her parents than anything else.

WINCE (wins) *v.* to flinch or tense your muscles due to pain

Mrs. Stein *winced* when she touched the hot stove.

WITNESS (wit-nis) *v.* to see or hear by being present

Liam *witnessed* a terrible car accident.

WITTY (wit-tee) *adj.* amusing and clever

Everyone laughed at Beth's *witty* remark.

Y

YIELD (yeeld) *v.* to give way

Mrs. Norris stopped her car, *yielding* to a duck that was crossing the road.

Z

ZEAL (zeel) *n.* enthusiasm for a person or a cause

The activists showed a lot of *zeal* when it came to saving the whales.

ANSWERS

QUIZ #1

1. O 2. S 3. S 4. S 5. O 6. O 7. S 8. O 9. S
10. S 11. O 12. O 13. O 14. S 15. O

QUIZ #2

1. S 2. S 3. O 4. S 5. O 6. S 7. O 8. O 9. O
10. S 11. S 12. O 13. S 14. O 15. S

QUIZ #3

1. c 2. b 3. d 4. a 5. c 6. b 7. d 8. a 9. c 10. d
11. c 12. b 13. c 14. b 15. a

QUIZ #4

1. T 2. F 3. F 4. F 5. T 6. F 7. F 8. T 9. T 10. T
11. F 12. T 13. T 14. T 15. T

QUIZ #5

1. c 2. e 3. o 4. m 5. i 6. j 7. a 8. b 9. n 10. f
11. k 12. h 13. l 14. g 15. d

QUIZ #6

1. k 2. b 3. m 4. h 5. n 6. a 7. e 8. l 9. o 10. d
11. c 12. f 13. i 14. j 15. g

QUIZ #7

1. S 2. O 3. S 4. S 5. S 6. O 7. O 8. S 9. O
10. S 11. O

QUIZ #8

1. S 2. S 3. O 4. S 5. O 6. S 7. O 8. O 9. S
10. S 11. S

QUIZ #9

1. c 2. b 3. a 4. c 5. b 6. a 7. d 8. a 9. b 10. c
11. d

QUIZ #10

1. d 2. h 3. g 4. i 5. e 6. f 7. b 8. c 9. i 10. a

QUIZ #11

1. a 2. e 3. d 4. h 5. f 6. g 7. c 8. b

QUIZ #12

1. a 2. c 3. b 4. a 5. d 6. c 7. a 8. d 9. b 10. a
11. d 12. b 13. d 14. a 15. b

QUIZ #13

1. g 2. o 3. a 4. h 5. f 6. n 7. b 8. j 9. c 10. l
11. m 12. d 13. i 14. e 15. k

QUIZ #14

1. g 2. i 3. l 4. b 5. d 6. n 7. a 8. o 9. m 10. f
11. k 12. h 13. j 14. e 15. c

QUIZ #15

1. T 2. F 3. F 4. T 5. T 6. F 7. T 8. F 9. F 10. F
11. T 12. T 13. T 14. F 15. F

QUIZ #16

1. S 2. S 3. O 4. S 5. O 6. O 7. O 8. S 9. O
10. O 11. S 12. O 13. S 14. S 15. O

QUIZ #17

1. O 2. S 3. S 4. O 5. S 6. O 7. S 8. O 9. O
10. S 11. O 12. O 13. S 14. O 15. S

QUIZ #18

1. S 2. S 3. O 4. O 5. S 6. S 7. O 8. O 9. O
10. S 11. S 12. S 13. O 14. O 15. S

QUIZ #19

1. c 2. a 3. d 4. a 5. c 6. d 7. b 8. d 9. a 10. d
11. a 12. b 13. c 14. b 15. a 16. d

QUIZ #20

1. j 2. g 3. n. 4. i 5. c 6. a 7. f 8. m 9. b 10. e
11. h 12. l 13. d 14. k

QUIZ #21

1. k 2. l 3. j 4. e 5. o 6. i 7. a 9. d. 10. b 11. f.
12. n 13. h 14. g 15. c

QUIZ #22

1. c 2. a 3. b 4. a 5. d 6. c 7. b 8. a 9. c 10. d
11. b 12. d 13. b 14. c 15. a 16. b 17. d 18. b
19. c 20. b

QUIZ #23

1. O 2. O 3. S 4. S 5. O 6. S 7. O 8. S 9. S 10. S
11. O 12. S 13. S 14. O 15. S 16. S 17. S
18. S 19. S 20. O

QUIZ #24

1. T 2. F 3. F 4. T 5. F 6. F 7. T 8. F 9. T 10. F
11. T 12. F 13. F 14. T 15. F 16. T 17. T 18. F

QUIZ #25

1. S 2. S 3. O 4. S 5. O 6. O 7. O 8. S 9. O
10. O 11. S 12. S 13. O 14. S 15. S 16. O
17. O 18. S 19. O 20. S

QUIZ #26

1. S 2. O 3. O 4. S 5. O 6. S 7. O 8. S 9. S
10. O 11. S 12. O 13. O 14. O 15. S 16. S
17. O 18. S 19. O 20. O

QUIZ #27

1. k 2. e 3. n 4. m 5. h 6. a 7. t 8. q 9. g 10. b
11. o 12. d 13. p 14. c 15. s 16. f 17. i 18. l
19. j 20. r

QUIZ #28

1. c 2. a 3. b 4. d 5. b 6. d 7. c 8. b 9. a 10. d
11. c 12. a 13. d 14. b 15. a 16. c 17. d 18. b
19. c 20. b

QUIZ #29

1. o 2. h 3. d 4. a 5. n 6. p 7. b 8. q 9. t 10. i
11. r 12. j 13. s 14. c 15. m 16. e 17. g 18. k
19. l 20. f

QUIZ #30

1. S 2. S 3. O 4. S 5. O 6. O 7. O 8. S 9. S
10. O 11. O 12. S 13. O 14. S 15. O 16. O
17. O 18. O 19. S 20. S 21. S 22. O 23. O
24. S 25. S 26. S 27. S

QUIZ #31

1. T 2. F 3. F 4. T 5. T 6. T 7. T 8. T 9. F 10. T
11. F 12. F 13. F 14. T 15. F 16. T 17. F
18. F 19. T 20. F 21. F 22. T 23. T 24. F 25. F

QUIZ #32

1. O 2. O 3. O 4. S 5. O 6. S 7. S 8. O 9. S
10. O 11. O 12. S 13. O 14. O 15. S 16. O 17. S
18. O 19. O 20. O 21. S 22. O 23. S 24. O
25. S 26. S 27. S 28. S 29. O 30. O

QUIZ #33

1. b 2. c 3. d 4. a 5. a 6. d 7. a 8. c 9. d 10. a
11. b 12. c 13. d 14. b 15. c 16. d 17. a 18. c
19. b 20. d 21. b 22. d 23. a 24. c 25. d

QUIZ #34

1. w 2. q 3. i 4. s 5. c 6. n 7. a 8. r 9. l 10. p
11. y 12. u 13. f 14. v 15. j 16. b 17. t 18. x
19. d 20. g 21. m 22. e 23. h 24. k 25. o

QUIZ #35

1. S 2. S 3. O 4. O 5. S 6. S 7. S 8. O 9. S
10. O 11. O 12. O 13. S 14. O 15. O 16. O
17. S 18. O 19. O 20. S 21. S 22. O 23. S
24. S 25. S 26. S 27. O 28. S 29. O

QUIZ #36

1. S 2. S 3. O 4. S 5. O 6. O 7. S 8. S 9. O
10. S 11. O 12. O 13. S 14. S 15. S 16. O 17. S
18. S 19. S 20. O 21. O 22. S 23. O 24. S 25. S

QUIZ #37

1. c 2. a 3. b 4. d 5. c 6. d 7. a 8. d 9. b 10. d
11. b 12. d 13. a 14. c 15. b 16. a 17. c 18. d
19. b 20. a 21. c 22. b 23. d 24. c

QUIZ #38

1. o 2. d 3. s 4. w 5. k 6. m 7. a 8. u 9. b 10. y
11. j 12. q 13. t 14. c 15. f 16. v 17. e 18. h 19. g
20. i 21. l 22. n 23. p 24. r 25. x

QUIZ #39

1. S 2. O 3. S 4. S 5. O 6. O 7. S 8. S 9. O
10. O 11. S 12. O 13. O 14. O 15. S 16. S 17. S
18. O 19. S 20. O 21. S 22. S 23. S 24. S

QUIZ #40

1. g 2. h 3. l 4. a 5. e 6. c 7. b 8. d 9. k 10. f
11 c 12. m 13. j

ABOUT THE AUTHOR

Hayley Heaton is a poet. Originally from Salt Lake City, Heaton was educated at the University of Utah and Cambridge University in England. She holds an M.F.A. in Creative Writing from The New School and currently lives in New York City. Her chapbook, *hubbub*, (Ahh Press) was published in 2004.

NOTES

NOTES

NOTES

NOTES

NOTES

NOTES

NOTES

NOTES

NOTES

NOTES

Award-Winning
SMART JUNIOR
Guides for Kids in Grades 6-8

Grammar Smart Junior, 3rd Edition
978-0-375-42870-8 • $13.95/$15.95 Can.

Math Smart Junior, 3rd Edition
978-0-375-42869-2 • $13.95/$15.95 Can.

Word Smart Junior, 3rd Edition
978-0-375-42871-5 • $13.95/$15.95 Can.

Word Smart Junior II, 2nd Edition
978-0-375-76258-1 • $12.00/$18.00 Can.

Writing Smart Junior, 2nd Edition
978-0-375-76261-1 • $12.00/$18.00 Can.

Winners of the Parents' Choice Award!